**Interpersonal Communication
in Organizations**

ORGANIZATIONAL AND OCCUPATIONAL PSYCHOLOGY

Series Editor: PETER WARR
*MRC Social and Applied Psychology Unit, Department of Psychology,
The University, Sheffield, England*

Theodore D. Weinshall
Managerial Communication: Concepts, Approaches and Techniques, 1979

Chris Argyris
Inner Contradictions of Rigorous Research, 1980

Charles J. de Wolff, Sylvia Shimmin, and Maurice de Montmollin
Conflicts and Contradictions: Work Psychology in Europe, 1981

Nigel Nicholson, Gil Ursell, and Paul Blyton
The Dynamics of White Collar Unionism, 1981

Dean G. Pruitt
Negotiation Behavior, 1981

Richard T. Mowday, Lyman W. Porter, and Richard M. Steers
Employee–Organization Linkages: The Psychology of Commitment,
Absenteeism, and Turnover, 1982

Richard A. Guzzo (Editor)
Improving Group Decision Making in Organizations: Approaches from
Theory and Research, 1982

George C. Thornton III and William C. Byham
Assessment Centers and Managerial Performance, 1982

Rudi Klauss and Bernard M. Bass
Interpersonal Communication in Organizations, 1982

Interpersonal Communication in Organizations

RUDI KLAUSS

*National Association of Schools of
Public Affairs and Administration
Washington, D.C.*

BERNARD M. BASS

*School of Management
State University of New York at Binghamton
Binghamton, New York*

1982
ACADEMIC PRESS
A Subsidiary of Harcourt Brace Jovanovich, Publishers
New York   London
Paris San Diego São Paulo Sydney Tokyo Toronto

ACADEMIC PRESS, INC.
111 Fifth Avenue, New York, New York 10003

United Kingdom Edition published by
ACADEMIC PRESS, INC. (LONDON) LTD.
24/28 Oval Road, London NW1 7DX

Library of Congress Cataloging in Publication Data

Klauss, Rudi.
   Interpersonal communication in organizations.

   (Organizational and occupational psychology)
   Includes bibliographical references and index.
   1. Communication in organizations.   2. Communication
in management.   I. Bass, Bernard M.   II. Title.
III. Series.
HD30.3.K585 1982   658.4'5   82-8847
ISBN 0-12-411650-7   AACR2

Contents

Preface

This began as a fairly straightforward study in management information systems. Interviews and survey data were collected from 400 project engineering personnel and supervisors in a light technology plant on the media, documents, and channels of communication that influenced their decision making. Almost 85% of the influence was attributed to face-to-face interpersonal interaction with co-workers. As a consequence, our focus shifted to interpersonal information transfer. We began to see that although substance was important, the style and credibility of the sender were a key to the impact of a message on a receiver. As a consequence, we have emerged with a book addressing the issue of interpersonal communication in organizational settings.

The book is concerned in particular with verbal communication behavior of managers and the perceptions and impact of such behavior on colleagues, including subordinates, peers, and superiors. Throughout, we have attempted to draw on prior research and have developed a model that is empirically examined in a variety of organizations. The strategy for collecting data from managers and their colleagues has combined a research emphasis with a feedback approach, which has enabled key participating managers to receive feedback concerning how their colleagues view them on specific dimensions of communication behavior. Thus, we have attempted to link prior research findings to our own research and at the same time provide an opportunity for learning to individuals who have provided the data reported in this volume.

We hope the book will be of interest to those who design and conduct communication training and to selected managers in various organizational settings. It also should be of use to students of communication in advanced undergraduate and graduate courses.

The effort that went into this book involved support and assistance from numerous sources and individuals during the past few years. Funding for much of the initial data collection and data analysis was made possible through an Office of Naval Research Contract (N0001476-C-0912). Many individuals also assisted us in this effort. Much of the computer analysis was performed at Syracuse University by John DeMarco, Robert McGowan, and Steve Loveless. Manuscript preparation was provided by Ann Goodwin. Finally, our families also deserve recognition for their continued understanding and support.

Interpersonal Communication
in Organizations

1

Introduction

Evil communications corrupt good manners.
—1 Corinthians, XV, 33

Good, the more
communicated, more abundant grows.
—*Paradise Lost*, Book IV, Line 71

Recognition of communication as the mediator of influence on behavior has been clear to the Gospel authors as well as to Milton. More important to us, however, is that communication is basic to organization. It links the organization's members. It mediates the inputs to the organization from the environment and the outputs from the organization to the environment (Guetzkow, 1965). In effect, it is "the very essence" of organizations (Katz & Kahn, 1966, p. 223). As Barnard (1938) suggested: "In the exhaustive theory of organization, communication would occupy a central place, because the structure, extensiveness, and scope of organization are almost entirely determined by communication techniques [p. 91]."

Despite the universal agreement concerning the importance of communication to organization, an understanding of how it actually operates within organizations remains elusive. Perhaps part of the reason is that communication is a substantive issue in a variety of widely disparate disciplines, such as sociology, electrical engineering, linguistics, psychology, physiology, mathematics, economics, speech, marketing, and information science. Each discipline adopts its own specific focus, and develops its own terminology and technology—with relatively little attention to other disciplines (Cherry, 1967; Thayer, 1967). Hence, learning from within each discipline is not fully exploited, although some interdisciplinary efforts, such as the application of the mathematics of information theory to the social psychology of communicating within organizations, are illustrative of what may be possible.

A more fundamental problem in studying communication, however, is that it is such a pervasive feature of organizations and thus is hard to isolate as a separate phenomenon for investigation (Porter & Roberts, 1976). As a result, progress toward improving our understanding of the nature and impact of communication within organizations has been slow. The amount of research being done in the area is steadily increasing. Nevertheless, more intensive, empirically based field research is needed.

In this book we concentrate on a particularly vital area—namely, the interpersonal communication of managers—drawing from several disciplines for concepts and techniques, particularly differential psychology, social psychology, sociology, and organizational behavior. More specifically, we examine the impact of differing manager communication styles on the attitudes and behavior of colleagues at work. After reviewing previously developed models and research, we construct a general model, then show how well it describes data we have collected in industry and government agencies. In addition, conditions that promote the effectiveness of different styles of interpersonal communication behavior are considered. In doing so, implications of these results for practicing managers and consultants in their day-to-day work are examined in turn.

Importance of Interpersonal Communication

Our concern with interpersonal communication at the managerial level is based on the view that managerial communication is probably one of the most critical areas of organizational communication in general and that it is the point at which managerial behavior can genuinely make a difference in influencing performance and employee attitudes. And if we consider the amount of time spent on communication on the part of managers, clearly its centrality to the manager's overall job cannot be denied. For example, Carlson (1951) conducted an intensive study of nine senior executives over a 4-week period and found that these senior managers spent approximately 80% of their time talking with others. In another intensive study of four departmental level managers, Burns (1954) also found that more than 80% of these managers' time was spent in conversation. Similar findings ranging from 70% to 80% have been reported across a spectrum of organization types and management levels (Goetzinger & Valentine, 1962; Lawler, Porter, & Tennenbaum, 1968; Lee & Lee, 1956; Mintzberg, 1973; Underwood, 1963). Thus, it is clear that an overwhelming amount of a manager's time is consumed by interpersonal communication. Moreover, such studies indicate that most of this communication occurs as oral, face-to-face interaction.

Given the importance of interpersonal communication, it is not surprising that competence in this area is ranked as very important by managers and executives themselves. For example, Murray (1976) asked a sample of public administrators at the state and local level across the United States to rank eight skills they felt young managers needed to perform effectively in public service. Communication skills (oral and written) ranked Number 1. In fact, 40 of the 70 respondents ranked communication skills as 1 or 2. When asked in what areas young professionals were generally most deficient, these respondents also ranked written and oral communications as the weakest area. Similar results have been reported in the private sector as well (Brickner, 1974).

Thus, it is evident that communication skills are among the more critical tools managers need to have in order to perform their jobs effectively. In fact, promotability may hinge to a considerable extent on competence in this area. It is certainly no accident, therefore, that we see considerable employment of group exercises and interviews in management assessment centers to test the proficiency of potential managers as communicators (Bray & Grant, 1966).

To summarize, communication clearly is a central phenomenon in organizations and is especially important for management. Certainly, as an activity it occupies a vast majority of a manager's time, and thus any increase in a manager's effectiveness or skill as a communicator should contribute directly or indirectly to improved organizational performance. The current state of knowledge in this area, however, is relatively fragmented, especially in terms of understanding specific behaviors that characterize effective interpersonal communication and the contribution that effective interpersonal communication can make to improving individual and organizational performance. We will focus on these issues and propose a framework for understanding the impact of a manager's interpersonal communication behavior in ongoing work organizations. It is hoped that this effort will contribute toward filling some of the gap in understanding that currently exists in this aspect of organizational behavior, and will in turn contribute to the eventual development of a contingency theory of interpersonal organizational communication that would suggest appropriate communication behaviors for given work contexts. In approaching these objectives, however, we must first briefly consider some boundary and definitional issues.

Boundary Issues

One of the major difficulties in studying communication is the ambiguity of the term itself. As Thayer (1967) notes, "communication may or may not be a single phenomenon; but certainly there is no universally accepted 'concept' of communication [p. 70]." Not only is the term ambiguous and multifaceted, but from a behavioral perspective, it appears to get at the essence of most every activity in work organizations. It can either characterize ongoing processes or be viewed as the precursor to individual employee behavior. As an example of the difficulty of drawing boundaries around communication, consider the potential overlap with leadership concerns. Leadership is influence. Influence requires effective communication. Leadership requires effective communication. Despite these connections, there is a surprising dearth of field or laboratory research on the linkages between leadership and communication behavior. Little has been done to describe the specific ways that particular communication styles relate to particular differences in leadership styles, even though, conceptually, various leadership styles have frequently been defined in terms of communication behaviors. Thus, Wofford, Gerloff, and Cummins (1977) suggest six basic styles of communication relevant to organizations: controlling, equalitarian, structuring, dynamic, relinquishing, and withdrawal. This list closely parallels frequently cited dimensions of leadership behavior. (We will further examine this important issue in an empirical way in Chapter 8.)

Communication and Information Processing

As the interplay of communication and leadership behavior indicates, it is difficult at best to separate communication from its organizational context and purpose as a discrete focus of attention. Perhaps in partial response to this difficulty, some studies have begun taking a communication and information processing perspective in describing and understanding behavior in organizational contexts (Hanser & Muchinsky, 1978; Nadler, 1977; Weick, 1969). Also illustrative of this perspective is the work of Rogers and Agarwala-Rogers (1976), who argue that "the behavior of individuals in organizations is best understood from a communication point of view [p. 3]."

Our approach here is sympathetic to a communication and information processing perspective, and we focus particularly on interpersonal verbal communication. Thus, we will not pay much attention to the preparation of formal written documents or to public speaking before large audiences within an organization or as a representative of an organization in the public arena. Rather, we are concerned with the more operational day-to-day communications between individual managers and their key personal communication links in the work setting (subordinates, peers, and supervisors), who form the primary, most intense network of communication ties for a focal manager in question. This is not say that other aspects of organizational communication are unimportant. However, since so much of a manager's time is spent in interpersonal verbal interaction, it seems reasonable to give this realm our primary attention. Thus, focal managers and verbal interactions in their immediate work settings, both at the dyadic (one-on-one) level and at the focal person's unit level (looking at multiple linkages between a focal person and the key colleagues who make up that person's communication net), constitute the principal focus of attention in this book.

Definitional Considerations

The supply of definitions of communication seems inexhaustible. For example, Dance (1970) identified 95 different versions. He was unable to extract a cohesive definition that adequately captured the multitude of perspectives toward this concept. Ultimately he concluded that "we are trying to make the concept 'communication' do too much for us [p. 210]." No attempt will be made here to cut quickly through this difficult problem, for no single succinct definition can meet all needs. Nevertheless, some clarification is required.

We start from the premise that interpersonal communication is a process, one that involves a minimum of two persons, sender and receiver. As such, it also entails communication contents (messages) that are transmitted by a selected medium or channel (face to face, telephone, written, etc.). Thus, a basic paradigm of sender–message–channel–receiver is seen here as the core of interpersonal communication processes.[1] In addition, one must also acknowledge a feedback component inherent in the communication process, thus making clear that communication is a dynamic ongoing process that has particular immediate outcomes for a receiver but also continues to influence subsequent communication activity (see Figure 1.1).

Given our concern in this book with verbal interpersonal communication in ongoing work organizations, we view the process of interpersonal communication in terms of messages and sentiments transmitted from one person to another with the expectation that such interaction will elicit some response from the receiver(s). The particular response may be immediate or delayed, direct or indirect, and involve attitude change, verbal reply, or other kinds of behavioral activity. However, in order for communication to occur or have meaning, it must register in some way with a receiver. It has to be *heard* as well as received.

Precisely because communication is a process rather than an out-

---

[1]Various versions of this basic paradigm have been presented in the literature. Thus, Berlo (1960) discusses a model incorporating a source, encoder, message, channel, decoder, and receiver. In the case of interpersonal communication, the encoding activity is performed by the source and the decoding occurs within the receiver, thus suggesting a more simplified interpersonal model of source → message → channel → receiver (S–M–C–R). Elsewhere, Lasswell (1948) proposed a similar verbal model in terms of *who* says *what* through what *channels* to *whom* with *what effect*. Alternative related models are discussed later in this chapter.

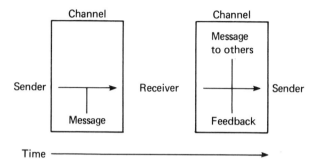

Figure 1.1. Basic interpersonal communication: sender–message–channel–receiver.

come, however, it remains an elusive and awkward phenomenon to study and understand. We will attempt to account for this in part by focusing on managerial *styles* of communication behavior that characterize the interpersonal communication process in specific work contexts. We recognize, however, that our approach does not inclusively capture the entire process involved, and we agree with Berlo (1960), who states:

> The important point is that we must remember that we are not including everything in our discussion. The things we talk about do not have to exist in exactly the same ways we talk about them. Objects which we separate may not always be separable and they never operate independently. This may appear obvious, but it is easy to overlook or forget the limitations that are necessarily placed on any discussion of a process [p. 24].

The Current State of the Art—Theory and Models

There is no shortage of books and articles about communication in organizations. However, most of these are hortatory admonitions on the art of speaking, writing, or listening. Systematic research in this area is surprisingly less voluminous than one might expect. Up to 1972, some 22 major studies constituted the bulk of the research reported in the area of organizational communication. This is in contrast to reports available for over 4000 investigations about job satisfaction (Porter & Roberts, 1976). This discrepancy in numbers makes clear the lack of attention given to this field as a subject of systematic inquiry. More discouraging, however, is the fact that research on communication in organizations has not grown very much since 1972. The situation has changed little from Guetzkow's (1965) review to Porter and Robert's (1976) follow-up. And there has been no dramatic increase in research since 1976.

In what immediately follows, we will look at communication from the perspective of organization theory. Then we will turn to communication models that have been developed to describe and analyze communication processes in organizational settings. Finally, we will consider major themes that emerge from a review of available surveys, experiments, and field studies to indicate the current state of the art in the field of interpersonal communication in organizations. The focus will be primarily on field studies carried out in work organizations, although some reference will also be made to laboratory research where appropriate. Major thrusts that have characterized research to date will be highlighted.[2]

Organization Theory Perspectives

"Theories are nets cast to catch what we call 'the world': to rationalize, to explain, and to master it. We endeavor to make the mesh ever finer and finer [Popper, 1959, p. 59]." As Popper notes, theories are developed in an attempt to capture the basic essence of that part of "reality" that is of concern to the researcher–theory builder. In a generic sense, the basic purpose of theory building then is to develop the capability to explain and predict. In the case of organization theory, this implies an ability to explain existing organizational behavior, to predict future organizational behavior, as well as to influence such behavior in selected ways. However, when one examines the current state of organization theory, it must be concluded that our capacity to explain, let alone predict, organizational behavior is still very limited. In terms of the above metaphor regarding theories, one might say that we are still trying to agree on exactly where to direct the casting of our nets. Moreover the size of the mesh is so large that a good deal of the essence continues to slip through and escape us. Hence, our ability to

[2]For additional extended coverage of research in the field, the reader is referred to the review articles of Guetzkow (1965), Thayer (1967), Barnlund (1968), Porter and Roberts (1976), Monge, Edwards, and Kirste (1978), and Goldhaber, Porter, Yates, and Lesniak (1978).

explain and predict organizational behavior is indeed in a state of infancy.

Nevertheless, it is still instructive to briefly consider what we can draw from organization theory to understand communication in organizations. Four categories of organization theory can be distinguished: classical theory; neoclassical, human relations approach; behavioral decision theory; and open systems theory.

CLASSICAL THEORY

Classical organization theory focused primarily on the structure, the division of work, and work units in organizations. Representative of one strand of classical theory was the effort of Taylor (1911), who was especially concerned with "scientific" ways of organizing work so that workers could carry out their assigned responsibilities more efficiently. Management's role was to establish efficient procedures and regulations that would specify exactly what and how workers were to do their jobs. Rigid adherence to such "scientifically" developed procedures was seen as the key to higher production. Hence, people became extensions of the machinery and technology around them, and the intent was to make them as efficient as possible in working with that machinery. From this point of view, organizational communication might best be seen in terms of a formalized system for relaying messages (commands, instructions, etc.) in a *downward* direction from manager to subordinate with no concern for upward feedback.

A second strand of classical organization theory, led by Fayol (1949), Weber (1947), Mooney and Reiley (1939), and Gulick and Urwick (1937), focused on issues of departmentalization—looking at how to structure the total organization formally into departmential units and subunits to get the job done effectively. Thus, whereas Taylor's work was directed more at the individual worker level and the physiological determinants of worker efficiency, this second strand, sometimes labeled administrative management theory, paid more attention to the problem of allocating and grouping task activities into work units that in turn could be structurally linked to each other through formalized chains of command. Of primary concern from this perspective was the division of labor, the scalar principle, functional processes, structure, and span of control. To the extent communication was dealt with by these theorists, it was in terms of flowing in the formalized channels that exist in the formal structure of the organization. Emphasis was given to downward communication to deal with issues of authority, delegation of responsibility, coordination, and control. For the most part, macroanalyses were dominant. Unfortunately, the basic principles outlined in these writings were so broad that the specific implications for understanding organizational communication, especially at the interpersonal level, are ignored. Thus, little concrete direction for developing a theoretical base to understand organizational communication (especially at the interpersonal level) is provided. Nevertheless, certain concerns stressed in this era have carried forward into later theory development and research. Some of these issues are treated in our own research reported in later chapters as we consider such factors as the effects of span of control, organizational level, and organization size on individuals and work units.

HUMAN RELATIONS THEORY

Organizational theories here focus on the "people side of the enterprise," the interpersonal and individual concerns in the work group. Whereas the classical theorists were primarily concerned with the formal structuring of work and of the organization, the neoclassical writers pay more attention to the informal organization that overlies the formal structure.

A major impetus to this line of thinking came from the Hawthorne studies (Roethlisberger & Dickson, 1939), and subsequent concern for the informal human dimension of organizational life is clearly revealed in the work of such writers as Argyris (1957, 1960), Likert (1961, 1967), and McGregor (1960). Implicit in the work of all these writers is a need for improving organizational communication in a climate of trust, openness, and through participation of subordinates in decision-making activities. However, less attention than might be expected is given directly to specifying a particular role for communication in increasing organizational effectiveness. In a sense, these writers all seem to recognize the importance of effective personal and organizational communication practices, but they are not particularly explicit concerning the specific elements and relationships involved. Nevertheless, their focus on the interpersonal dimension has suggested fruitful areas of research that could help clarify the relationship of interpersonal communication behavior to other organizational variables. Clearly, we will draw on concepts and techniques stressed in the human relations theory and research in the development of our model and in the consideration of such issues as trust, openness, and interaction potential between senders and receivers.

BEHAVIORAL DECISION THEORY

The behavioral decision approach is seen in the works of Simon (1945, 1957), March and Simon (1958), and Cyert and March (1963). Central to much of their work is the principle of "bounded rationality," which posits that people have limits to their ability to comprehend their environment and that consequently we can expect individuals to operate rationally only within the context of, or relative to, a frame of reference that is determined by the limitations of their knowledge and information processing capabilities.

Thus, these writers do consider communication and the information processing capabilities of managers as key issues in understanding organizational behavior. Communication in this context is seen to play an important role in transmitting procedures to workers and as a tool or mechanism to reduce uncertainty within organizations. However, their view tends to be somewhat mechanistic in that little attention is given to critical individual and interpersonal dynamics that ultimately figure into the communication process.

In later chapters we draw on some of the concerns addressed in this literature and attempt to make some linkages between such issues as the information processing demands of the work environment and communication behavior that occurs at the interpersonal level.

OPEN SYSTEMS THEORY

In the open systems theory, organizations are seen in dynamic interaction with their environments. Whereas traditional approaches toward organizations have taken a somewhat mechanistic, internally focused, and static view of organizations, current writers see organizations as probabilistic, organic, open systems attempting to develop internal organizational mechanisms to cope with a complex, dynamic environment. Representative of this perspective is the work of Katz and Kahn (1966; 1978), Thompson (1967), Weick (1969), Lawrence and Lorsch (1967), and Pfeffer and Salancik (1978).

Implicit in this perspective is a recognition that communication plays an important linking role in enabling the organization to sense its environment more accurately and convey information concerning the environment to appropriate information processing points within the organization so that the organization can cope more effectively with the uncertain environmental context within which it operates. Internally, organizational communication helps to further protect and direct the central core processes through formal and more spontaneous channels, which in turn can help the organization respond to and anticipate the external environment. The importance of roles and role linkages in clarifying organizational relationships and communication processes can be seen to further enable organizations and their members to deal with the generalized uncertainty they face. From this perspective, organizational communication is a source for increasing goal and role clarity over time. Thus, these writers do focus on information and communication requirements of organizations, especially at the macro level. However, the linkage to microlevel managerial communication behavior as it affects colleagues is not well developed as yet, except as may be inferred from Likert's (1967) "linking pin" concept to understanding organizations.

Our own model builds extensively on the ideas developed in this literature by focusing on the linkages between communicators and their various colleagues (peers and superiors as well as subordinates) and by casting the communication process in a contingency context in which demands external to the work unit (such as technology constraints, size factors, and other forces) may require variations in communication behavior among colleagues in the immediate work setting.

This sketch of organization theory in relation to communication suggests increasing concern for the role of effective communication in organizations. There is an implicit recognition that communication channels and flow are somehow involved in the functioning of organizations. And yet, organization theory for the most part does not directly address organizational communication per se as a fundamental variable for understanding and explaining organizational behavior. Hence, we are inclined to agree with Porter and Roberts (1976) that much more work needs to be done in developing a theoretical basis for viewing communication in organizations.

Communication Theory and Models

Here we find material more directly relevant to organizational communication. A number of influential models and theories to explain the communication process are available.[3]

---

[3]For a more detailed and extensive discussion of the range of models in the literature, the reader is referred to reviews by Johnson and Klare (1961), Thayer (1967), Barnlund (1968), and Cherry (1966).

One of the earliest and most influential models comes from work in the field of telecommunications research (Shannon, 1948; Shannon & Weaver, 1949). Shannon and Weaver proposed the paradigm shown in Figure 1.2 to describe the communication process.

This information processing model subsequently attracted a great deal of attention, particularly for its potential to measure the amount of information transmitted. However, the model did not prove helpful to researchers concerned with the social–interpersonal dimension of communication (Porter & Roberts, 1976). Indeed, Chapanis (1971) went so far as to argue that, for those interested in communication in a social context, the literature on communication–information theory is essentially useless.

A model that focused more directly on the interpersonal processes involved in communication was needed. Newcomb (1953) originated one in simplest form. Interpersonal communication occurs when Person A transmits something about object x to Person B. Westley and MacLean (1957) extended this model in their work on mass communication by including an additional element, C (a filter of sorts), which selects abstractions of object x that it translates into symbolic form and transmits via some channel to the receiver (Person B). Dance (1967) proposed a helical model of interpersonal communication that emphasized that communication while moving forward is also feeding back on itself and is being influenced by past behavior. More complex models, such as Barnlund's (1968), further delineated various procesesses, such as decoding, encoding, nonverbal, and behavioral cues, that influenced the communication process.

It became possible to include organizational considerations when

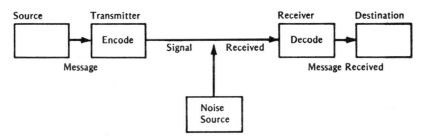

Figure 1.2. Shannon and Weaver (1949) model of communication.(From C. Shannon & W. Weaver, *The mathematical theory of communication.* Urbana: University of Illinois Press. Copyright 1949 by University of Illinois Press.)

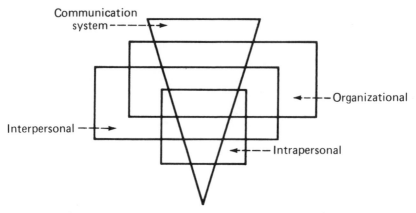

Figure 1.3. Levels of organizational communication and their interfaces. (From L. Thayer, *Communication and communication systems.* Homewood, Illinois: Irwin, 1968, p. 271.)

Thayer (1967, 1968) added another dimension to the study of communication processes by pointing out the crucial importance of differentiating levels of analysis when considering communication processes. He suggested three important levels (intrapersonal, interpersonal, and organizational) which along with technological communication factors combined to form a hybrid level of analysis that he labeled the communication systems level (Figure 1.3). In differentiating these levels, he noted that we need to be careful to recognize that each level has its own unique set of dynamics and that we must also be prepared to look at the interface of these levels when we study communication in organizations.

The concern for differentiating levels of analysis in studying organizational communication was also stressed by Roberts, O'Reilly, Bretton, and Porter (1974), who noted "that communication operates somewhat differently at various levels of organizational analysis [p. 514]." They in turn argued for a multilevel approach (individual, internal organizational, organizational–environmental) to the study of communication.

Still another orientation was proposed by Morris (1946), who cast the study of communication in terms of a theory of signs. Three different sets of issues have to be considered: (*a*) syntactic issues (the relationship between signs, abstracted from the user): (*b*) semantic issues (the relationship between signs and the things, actions, relationship, and qualities they are meant to represent); (*c*) pragmatic issues (the relationship between signs and their users).

Of these efforts that represent various approaches taken in the study of communication, each captures some of the communication process and context. However, none fully explains the nature of the communication process in organizational settings, particularly its interpersonal aspects. Thus, despite the considerable effort in constructing communication models and approaches to understanding the process, we are inclined to agree with Thayer, who notes: "Perhaps more has been 'communicated' about 'communication problems' in organizations than any other single topic in the field. Yet this plethora of commentary has not been conducive either to theory building or to theory validation [1967, p. 80]." More than a decade later, little further progress had been made.

It is our hope and expectation in terms of the need expressed in the preceding discussion that a more complex model can be developed and tested that captures much more of the idiosyncratic nature of interpersonal communication in organizational contexts.

Empirical Research

Concrete, research-based knowledge about communication stems mainly from laboratory experiments and a smattering of field studies. As noted by Weinshall (1979), most of such research is based either on perceptions of those being studied or on observations made by others. Knowledge coming from the various empirical studies based on these strategies can be divided into three general catagories: the context of the communication, content–process issues, and outcomes. The context of communication involves the setting within which a sender communicates (e.g., status of sender, trust in sender, work group size, technology, level within the organization). The content–process category focuses primarily on such issues as the direction of flow, quality, amount, timeliness of the communication, as well as channel characteristics. The outcomes category incorporates concerns with the potential impact or effects of communication on individuals, work groups, and the larger organization (e.g., attitudes, performance).

This threefold categorization helps to order our thinking toward the focus on outcomes and impacts that directs the overall thrust of this book. As we move on to subsequent chapters, the rationale for this approach will become even more evident. Moreover, it places the communication process into a contingency framework that recognizes that communication activity will vary considerably across situations and will have differing impact as well, depending on the immediate context. Thus, as we proceed in this discussion, we will bear in mind the contingent nature of communication and the fact that the impact, content–process dimensions, and contextual factors are to a certain extent mutually interactive.

The Context of Communication

The context of interpersonal communication includes factors that are relatively objective, such as organizational structure, technology of work situation, size of organizational units, hierarchical level, physical proximity, and education level of the sender. It also includes subjective interpersonal dimensions, such as perceived trustworthiness and influence of communicator, mobility aspirations, and general organizational climate. Both objective and subjective variables have been shown to relate differently to communication processes and outcomes.

STRUCTURE

The term *structure* generally is used to describe the formal or required hierarchical and lateral linkages between organizational positions. It includes the bureaucratic and physical constraints on communications required or permitted between occupants of the positions in the organization.

The effects of structure and control of communications have been the subject of a long line of laboratory investigation. In such research, various kinds of structures were imposed on small groups performing tasks ranging from simple, routine activities to more complex problems. A common finding was that for simple tasks a centralized structure (as, for example, in a star-shaped network where communication is restricted to two-way flows between a central person and those at the peripheries of the star) was associated with high performance (as measured by speed and accuracy of problem solution). This compared with decentralized, unrestricted structural nets (all-channel) where everyone could communicate with everyone else. However, while performance tended to be better in the star condition, satisfaction and morale tended to be lower than for the all-channel situation (Bavelas & Barrett, 1951; Leavitt, 1951). With more complex tasks, however, the performance difference between star and all-channel tended to disappear. In fact, decentralized structures sometimes outperformed centralized ones (Lawson, 1965; Shaw, 1954). Meanwhile, morale remained higher for the all-channel condition.

Subsequent research (Burgess, 1969; Snadowsky, 1972) provided further clarification of these early findings. In particular, Burgess noted that differences in performance between different structures tended to disappear once groups had worked under a given configuration for a period of time and had attained a steady state—particularly when reinforcement was used. Later research suggested that, when communication was restricted as in groups led in an authoritarian style, such groups took less time to plan than did unstructured groups. However, the former were less efficient in accomplishing tasks (Snadowsky, 1972).

In short, these various laboratory studies suggested that various structures and their resultant communication networks did appear to affect performance differentially under certain conditions but that over time many of these differences in performance seemed to wash out. However, high morale and satisfaction were usually associated with unrestricted, open communication. The implication for ongoing work organizations is that creating structures to increase communication flow is likely to enhance satisfaction and, for more complex task environments, performance as well.

In addition to these laboratory studies, a number of field studies underscore important relationships between structure and communication. Looking at structure from a total organization perspective, for example, Burns and Stalker (1961) found that a mechanistic organizational structure (where positions and interrelationships among positions are fixed and unchanging) was characterized by vertical communication patterns with decisions centered at top levels. In contrast, *organic* firms with less rigidity defined positions tended more toward lateral communication patterns. Overall structure may also affect the quality and nature of vertical communication. For instance, Wilensky (1967, pp. 44–77) notes that the nature of hierarchical structure (number of levels, shape of hierarchy) affects the flow of information. A general response to hierarchical constraints is for communication to occur outside formal channels. Moreover, hierarchical distinctions very often appear to be associated with the accuracy and amount of information that is passed, especially in an upward direction (Athanassiades, 1973, 1974; Level & Johnson, 1978; O'Reilly & Roberts 1974, 1977; Read, 1962). Elsewhere, complexity of organizational structure (as measured by variety of occupations and amount of professional activity) has also been shown to correlate positively with intensity of communication in general and with horizontal communication in particular (Hage, Aiken, & Marrett, 1971).

Looking at structure in terms of where one sits in the overall hierarchy may also be important. Bacharach and Aiken (1977) examined structural constraints on frequency of communication by departmental heads and subordinates in 44 local government bureaucracies and found that structural constraints (size, shape, decentralization, and boundary spanning) were more important in predicting frequency of communication among lower level personnel than for middle level bureaucrats. These results suggest the importance of clarifying the level under study within the organization when examining communication processes. This view is supported by other research (Davis, 1953; Sutton & Porter, 1968), which indicates that hierarchical level influences the nature and content of grapevine (informal) communication and the kind of information filtration that occurs (Davis, 1968).

Looking at the impact of structure on mode or channel of communication at a micro task group level, Allen and Cohen (1969) found that in a research and development (R&D) setting the formal organizational structure was more important than the social structure in conveying technical information, but was by no means the sole determinant of such communication in the laboratory. That is, the social (informal) structure as well as the formal work structure interacted in facilitating technical communication flows. In terms of specific modes of communication, Conrath (1973b) found that written communication patterns were associated with the authority structure, telephone communication with the task structure, and face-to-face interaction with the physical structure. We propose to look at the impact of structure in our analysis in Chapter 6.

PROXIMITY

While the preceding dimensions of structure focus particularly on issues related to chain of command, decision making, and authority relations, structural constraints imposed by physical distance have also been shown to influence communication behavior. For example, Gullahorn (1952) found that greater distance between work locations of clerical personnel led to less communication. In a year long study of the impact of a "nonterritorial" office layout, Allen and Gerstberger (1973) observed that communication among product engineers was significantly higher with this arrangement than with the traditional floor arrangements (office walls and permanent work stations). Employees preferred this new arrangment. However, departmental performance did not change measurably. Again, Hage (1974) found that the more an organization is physically dispersed, the greater the average intensity of committee and departmental meetings as well as the amount of unscheduled communications. He observed that "what is perhaps most interesting is that the frequency of interactions within physically dispersed departments are decreased while those between physically dispersed departments are increased [p 218]." Thus, the physical spread seemed to create a greater need for coordination as shown by increased communication volume between organizational subsystems physically scattered about. This pattern of findings is consistent with a view expressed by Barnlund and Harland (1963), who suggested that physical factors may hamper interpersonal communication initially but that over time the evolving social structure can compensate for physical barriers. Also, the availability of alternative modes of communication (written, telephone, face to face) helps to overcome distance factors (Conrath, 1973a). The effects of proximity in our investigations will be examined in Chapter 5.

Caveats. Three observations can be made from these studies concerning structure and proximity. First, it is clear that the concept of structure has taken on several meanings and has been measured in numerous ways in the literature. While this reflects the complexity of organizations in general and the multifaceted nature of structure in particular, it also limits our ability to make comparisons across research studies. Thus, to generalize about structural impacts on communication without carefully considering how this construct is being defined and measured in particular studies is hazardous at best.

Second, it does seem evident that structural features (no matter how defined and operationalized) consistently do influence communication in several ways (e.g., amount, quality, channel selection, satisfaction, and occasionally performance). Conceptual fuzziness and theoretical gaps may muddy the interpretation of such findings, but a general pattern is there. What is needed is further conceptual work to forge linkages among various dimensions of structure if we are to appreciate fully its impact on communication.

Third, while most research views communication as a consequence of structuring (or as operating within a structural constraint), we should not exclude consideration of a reverse relationship—namely, that communication processes may also determine structure (Rogers & Agarwala-Rogers, 1976). Thus, in certain instances, communication needs (personal as well as task related) may "cause" individuals to establish certain communication patterns, which in turn may become more formalized and structured over time through reorganization of the formal structure to compensate for gaps in the existing structure or through the creation of informal structures to take up the slack. To some extent, the study by Allen and Gerstberger (1973) and other experiments in office landscaping represent tendencies in this direction. However, this approach to the relationship between structure and communication has been largely neglected to date.

SIZE EFFECTS

As with structure, organization size has been variously defined and measured and has usually been treated as an antecedent or constraint or communication behavior. Most studies operationalize size in terms of number of employees, although other measures, such as net assets, sales volume, and number of clients, are also occasionally utilized. As Kimberly (1976) points out, however, the rationale for employing a particular measure of size is usually not very well developed in most research. Nevertheless, size has been shown to have considerable impact on communication behavior. For example, in a review of 31 empirical studies (mostly laboratory experiments), Thomas and Fink (1963) concluded that group size has significant effects on the nature of interaction and the distribution of participation of group members.

Studies in organizational settings tend to confirm these general findings. Size was shown to be positively correlated with amount of subordinate communication in all directions (Bacharach & Aiken, 1977). Elsewhere, Blau (1968) found that the ratio of operating personnel to managers in an organization had an impact on upward communication opportunities and communication feedback. Other field research suggests that as work group size increases there is a corresponding increase in lateral communication and decrease in face-to-face interaction (Roberts & O'Reilly, 1974a).

In many instances, the level of analysis in examining the relationship of size to individual communication behavior would be the work group. However, other size considerations (number and size of departments, as well as total organization size) might also influence the intensity and direction of flow. The relative importance and interactions between these levels of analysis has not been systematically examined. This point is confirmed by Porter and Lawler (1965, p. 39), who have noted that "investigators have failed to control for variation in size of the other types of subunits (primary work-groups, department, large organization) of which the individual is a member while they are studying the effects of size on one type of unit."

Despite rather consistent findings linking size to communication behavior, much research is still called for. The differential effects of levels of analysis need exploration, as do questions concerning the general assumption of linear relationships between size and effects on communication. For example, Blau and Schoenherr (1971) found a curvilinear relationship between size and certain organization structure variables such as, division of labor and number of sections per division. The curve began to flatten noticeably for agencies exceeding 1000 employees. Elsewhere, Hall, Haas, and Johnson (1967), in a study of 75 organizations, found inconsistent relationships between size and structural characteristics for small (less than 100 employees), medium (100–999 employees), and large organizations (1000 or more employees). It might be that once total organization size reaches a certain level, its impact on communication diminishes as other factors take over in importance (number of departments, work unit size, or such other considerations as work flow and overriding technology contraints). Comstock and Scott (1977), for example, concluded that, while size may have a separate effect on subunit structure, it is a less powerful predictor than technology. The effects of size in our data analysis will be examined in Chapters 5 and 6.

TECHNOLOGY EFFECTS

It is difficult to separate technology's effects from those of size and structure (Gerwin, 1979; Hickson, Pugh, & Pheysey, 1969; Mohr, 1971). That is, you cannot have a very small steel mill or casually run backyard furnaces. An additional issue surrounding the technology question is the level at which technology is (or should be) measured or classified. Much of the reported research tends to place entire organizations into one category or another for purposes of analysis (Woodward, 1965), although other studies suggest that such macro-level categorizations may make unrealistic assumptions of homogeneity between departmental units and subunits (horizontally and vertically) within the larger organization being categorized (Comstock & Scott, 1977).

Apart from the level of analysis question, there is also the issue of conceptualizing technology in a standard way. Woodward (1965), for example, employed a threefold scheme for characterizing industrial organizations: unit production, mass production, and process production. Subsequently, Thompson (1967) proposed another classification scheme: long linked technologies, mediating technologies, and intensive technologies. Both classification schemes noted differences in required communication patterns. At a more operational level, many research studies have taken degree of technical certainty, predictability, and routineness of tasks as measures in differentiating technological demands of the work situation with consequential effects on communication. Research examining the relationships between technology and communication still tends to be neglected (Porter & Roberts, 1976). Nevertheless, Randolph and Finch (1977) showed that technology measured in terms of task uncertainty was directly proportional to horizontal communication and inversely related to vertical communication and frequency of task communication. Van de Ven, Delbecq, and Koening (1976) also found that, as perceived task uncertainty increased, horizontal communication, as well as frequency of scheduled and unscheduled meetings, increased. However, there was no effect on vertical communication. Elsewhere, Penley (1977) reported that routinization and analyzability of task were key factors in differentiating between five types of communication clusterings. Pelz and Andrews (1976) found that in R&D settings higher performing scientists generally had a greater degree of contact with colleagues outside their work group but within the organization. Other research in R&D settings has suggested that the more successful projects adjust their communication processes to match the information processing demands of the work and that the more effective managers actively manage communication processes to suit project demands (Katz & Tushman, 1979; Tushman, 1978).

Several studies have noted that most communications in innovative organizational units are frequently handled by a limited number of key members in a work group who can be viewed as gatekeepers and organization liaisons (Allen, 1966; Allen & Cohen, 1969; Tushman, 1977). In this connection, Holland (1972) reported that persons in R&D settings who served as key information focal points utilized a more diverse set of external information sources and had an unusually large number of acquaintances or read an above-average amount of external reference material (journals, reports, etc.). Whitley and Frost (1973) further delineated four types of scientific work (responsibility tasks, extension tasks, new development tasks, and basic research) and found that task type was related to information source usage patterns.

In sum, these studies suggest that technology does in fact influence communication patterns and processes in important ways and that in the more complex technology environments special communication roles and needs frequently emerge to compensate for and deal with the increasing uncertainty or lack of predictability of the work. We will look at communication in two organizations with different technologies in Chapter 6.

INTRAPERSONAL AND INTERPERSONAL FACTORS

Up to now, our discussion of the context of communication has focused on characteristics or properties of the task and organization that may constrain or influence interpersonal communication. These are largely the givens or objective constraints within which communication occurs. There is a second set of contextual variables, however, which inhere in the persons involved in the communication process. These factors involve the personal attributes of senders and receivers and their perceptions of each other and the immediate interpersonal environment.

Trust. Among variables that fall into this category, interpersonal trust is one of the most frequently researched dimensions. Generally, it has been established that trust influences the quality, level, content, and directionality of communication. For example, Zand (1972) conducted a business simulation involving middle and upper level managers in which trust was manipulated. Managers were placed in high- or low-trust problem solving groups. Zand found highly significant differences between high-trust and low-trust groups. The high-trust groups exchanged relevant ideas and feelings more openly, developing greater clarity in goals and problems, searched for more alternative courses of action, and were more committed to implement solutions. In another laboratory experiement, O'Reilly and Roberts (1974) found that senders altered the direction of information and filtered information depending on their trust in the receivers. Trust especially affected upward information flow.

Similar findings have been reported in field studies. Thus, trust has been shown to be an important aspect of willingness to communicate (Mellinger, 1956; Roberts & O'Reilly, 1974b; Walton, 1962). It also affects perceptions of communication accuracy (O'Reilly & Roberts, 1976). Read (1962) found trust to be moderator of upward communication. Communication was actually more accurate under conditions of high trust. O'Reilly (1978) provides additional evidence concerning the trust–accuracy relationship based on several laboratory and field studies. Overall, the results indicate a general tendency to screen unfavorable and sharpen favorable information sent in upward directions. Lack of trust significantly increased this tendency.

Thus, there is little question that personal trust and interpersonal communication tendencies are strongly related. Most studies imply trust causes the resultant communication behavior. Yet, one may ask whether a reverse sequence or mutual interaction is not also possible. In other words, it seems plausible that better quality communication (accuracy, less filtration, openness, etc.) may increase the level of trust among colleagues. This issue has not been dealt with very well in the research to date. Another qualification to the research reported to date is that trust has been measured in a number of different ways. Giffin (1967), for example, draws on studies relating to source credibility and suggests several components for consideration: expertness, reliability, activeness, personal attraction, and majority opinion views as to extent a communicator should be trusted. More recently, source credibility has been factor analytically defined in terms of three components— safety or overall trustworthiness, expertise, and dynamism (Berlo, Lemert, & Mertz, 1969–1970)—and these measures have been applied in field research studies (Falcione, 1974; O'Reilly & Roberts, 1974). In the model to be presented and tested in the chapters that follow, these three measures of credibility will be seen as intervening variables that alter the effects of communications on receiver's motives and needs.

Motives and Needs. Another interpersonal contextual factor related to communication behavior involves the internal motivations of organization members. Thus, the amount of technical communications sent has been predicted by such personal attributes as an innovative orientation, a lack of need for clarity and personal growth, and a desire for relatedness. However, none of these personal attributes predicted the tendency to send managerial or administrative communications (Keller & Holland, 1978). Elsewhere, mobility aspirations of individuals have been related to accuracy of upward communication, although this was moderated by interpersonal trust—that is, where high trust existed, communication was more accurate (Read, 1962). Athanassiades (1973) similarly found that subordinate tendencies to screen, withhold, and distort was influenced by ascendency and security needs. O'Reilly (1978), however, found that persons with strong mobility aspirations engaged in less information distortion and generally concluded that for the samples under consideration this variable was of little importance. In Chapters 5 and 8, we will attempt to see the extent actual mobility plays a role in communications to others.

Similarity. An additional interpersonal contextual issue relates to the extent to which senders and receivers of communications are similar to each other in certain attributes such as beliefs, values, and education. A prevalent view has been that high degrees of similarity between sender and receiver (homophily) will facilitate communication flows and understanding. Triandis (1959), for example, obtained evidence to suggest that cognitive similarity facilitates interpersonal communication and liking. More recently, researchers have begun to ask the question "homophily with respect to what" (Rogers & Bhowmik, 1971; Simons, Berkowitz, & Moyer, 1970). This question may be especially pertinent in situations where new ideas or innovations are being proposed (Rogers & Agarwala-Rogers, 1976, pp. 115–116). Hence, the homophily–heterophily issue and its consequences for communication effectiveness is clearly quite complex. In fact, it may be more appropriate to think in terms of "optimal heterophily" (Alpert & Anderson, 1973), contingent on the individuals involved, the work situation, and specific information needs and messages.

Demographic variables, such as age, education, and seniority of communicators, have also been considered in research on communication. Thus, Lawrence (1972) found that older managers (for samples of lower middle managers in 11 different companies) reported greater frequency of all forms of communication from higher management and significantly fewer barriers. Keller and Holland (1978) found that age and organizational level were significant predictors of administrative and managerial communication but not of innovative and technical communication. Education, on the other hand, predicted innovative—technical communication but not managerial–administrative communication.

Such factors as age, education, and seniority, however, present some difficulties in that they may not represent critical distinctions of importance. For example, education may in some instances act somewhat as a surrogate for status or other considerations. Thus, Allen (1967) found that in small R&D labs PhDs formed tightly knit groups and seldom met with non-PhDs socially or regarding technical matters. In this instance, education may have taken on a status value, which in turn influenced communication patterns. Similarly, age and seniority may incorporate many interrelated elements, including experience, organizational level, and motivational needs (Goldhaber, Porter, Yates, & Lesniak, 1978). Such considerations and possible explanations of communication processes have sometimes been neglected in interpreting research. In Chapter 5, we will attempt to encompass the effects on communication of any of these personal congruences between senders and receivers using the concept of interaction potential (Bass, 1960), which argues for more communication when the congruence is greater.

Content and Process Effects on Communication

The preceding discussion has focused on a number of factors that provide the context for interpersonal communication. They constitute the setting within which interpersonal processes occur. A second broad set of issues surrounding interpersonal communication pertain to the way communications occur and the content of such exchanges. Thus, the concern here is more with *what* is communicated and how it flows, as well as with other related characteristics of the communication process (timeliness, amount, quality, filtering, direction, etc.). Some of these variables have already been referred to in relation to particular contextual variables, but in this section we take the process–content issues as a principal focus and relate them to additional variables of concern in the literature on organizational communication.

CHANNEL CHOICE AND USE

Among various factors included in this section, the issue of communication channel choice and use has been quite extensively researched. Various studies have indicated that managers rely more heavily on verbal channels than on written ones (Burns, 1954; Carlson, 1951; Lee & Lee, 1956; Mintzberg, 1973). Moreover, face-to-face interaction is frequently preferred and more satisfying than telephone communication (Conrath, 1973a; Housel & Davis, 1977; Weinshall & Shalev, 1979).

A number of factors may help to explain the extent to which particular channels are used. Thus, as noted before, channel choice has been shown to relate to organizational structure, with face-to-face interaction associated primarily with physical structure, telephone communication with task structure, and written communication with authority structure (Conrath, 1973b). Contrary to general wisdom, channel quality (quality of information, relative number of acceptable ideas) is not necessarily related to channel choice (Allen, 1966). Gerstberger and Allen (1968), for example, found that perceived accessibility of information channels was most strongly related to frequency of channel use (as compared to three other criteria—ease of use, technical quality, and degree of experience). Another factor that may influence channel choice and use is the organizational and communication climate. Thus, Dewhirst (1971) found that the use of interpersonal (verbal) channels was higher when the information sharing norm was higher, whereas written communication appeared to take up the slack for reduced interpersonal communication when the information sharing was low. In Chapters 5, 7, and 8, we will further examine causes and effects of channel choice.

INTERPERSONAL CHANNELS AS INFORMATION SOURCES

Communication channels are also characterized as information sources in various studies. Thus, O'Reilly (1977) found that decision making by subordinates was improved with more frequent use of supervisors as information sources. Allen (1969) indicated the importance of interpersonal sources as central information inputs and suggested that perhaps too much attention is given to improving the efficiency of impersonal channels. This view is supported by the importance of "technological gatekeepers" or "liaisons," who have been shown to act as vital links across groups within organizations and to the external environment (Davis, 1953; Sutton & Porter, 1968).

AMOUNT OF COMMUNICATION

Another communication process issue involves the amount and frequency of communication exchanges as independent variables (as causes rather than as effects). For example, Randolph and Finch (1977) found an inverse relationship between frequency of task communication and certainty of technology. In a study focusing on engineers and scientists in R&D laboratories, Pelz and Andrews (1976) found that those persons with above-average contact (up to a certain point) tended to perform at higher levels than those with less contact. Nevertheless, attempts to merely increase the amount of communication may not prove beneficial in all cases. Thus, in R&D settings, for example, "it may be important to solidify interpersonal relationships and communications with particular individuals and areas rather than trying to establish a broad spectrum of organizational contacts [Katz & Tushman, 1979, p. 160]." In later chapters, we will examine how amount and quality of communications affect productivity and satisfaction.

DIRECTION

Numerous studies concerning the direction of communication flows have also been reported. As mentioned earlier, various studies reveal a tendency to filter upward communication depending on mobility aspirations and trust (Level & Johnson, 1978; O'Reilly & Roberts, 1974; Read, 1962). However, downward communication may also be filtered and distorted (Brenner & Sigband, 1973; Davis, 1968). In Chapter 5, we will focus on the effects of organizational level differences on communication patterns.

Horizontal communication also plays an important role in organizations. Thus, Randolph and Finch (1977) found a direct relationship between technological certainty and proportion of organization members engaging in horizontal communication. Elsewhere, Albaum (1964) noted that horizontal flows of unsolicited information were overly restricted.

MESSAGE CONTENT

Little research has differentiated communication content. Generally, the assumption is that the communication is immediately task–job specific or at least has direct implications for the immediate work situation, but the relative efficiency of alternative channels in communicating different kinds of job-related information is an area that has been largely neglected. A few exceptions to this pattern can be found, however. The early work of Davis (1953) gave clues in this direction, suggesting that the grapevine was a central mechanism for communicating organizational information. Sutton and Porter (1968), in a subsequent study of the grapevine in a government agency, found that the transmission of information increased somewhat when it was more task relevant.

Looking more directly at channel use and message content, Davis (1968) found that routine parking information was poorly communicated orally down the managerial hierarchy, whereas critical production-oriented layoff information was very well communicated via oral communication channels. These findings suggest that high-interest, critical information is frequently more appropriate for oral chain of command to lower organizational levels, whereas routine, noncritical information (e.g., parking) has a better probability of reaching lower levels through a written medium. This also frees up managers for more critical communications via oral channels. One of the most direct attempts to relate communication channel (oral, written, or in combination) to specific types of messages is reported by Level (1972). In this study, 72 business supervisors were asked to evaluate four methods of communicating (written only, oral only, written followed by oral, and oral followed by written) against 10 situations frequently encountered in the work place (situations requiring immediate employee action, situations requiring future action, communicating general information, transmitting a company order, policy change, communicating to an immediate supervisor about work progress, promoting a safety campaign, commending outstanding employee work, reprimanding poor work, settling a work dispute between employees). In general, oral followed by written was seen as the most effective. One problem with this study, however, is that it rests on supervisors' judgments of relative effectiveness of various approaches across situations without actually testing for behavioral impacts on the part of those receiving the communication. This is an area needing further attention. We will partially address the problem in Chapters 5, 7, and 8.

Outcomes of Communication

A third set of variables with which communication research has been concerned includes the impacts of communication exchanges on individuals, groups, and the larger organization. Such outcomes incorporate attitudinal measures, such as satisfaction with the communicator, job, and organization, as well as behavioral outcomes, such as performance, turnover, and absenteeism. While much of the research in this area generally seems implicitly to presume that communication behavior "causes" particular outcomes, the research designs in most instances are cross-sectional correlation studies in which directionality is not specifically tested. Hence, care must be taken in the interpretation of research results.

SATISFACTION AND COMMUNICATION

Several studies have looked at the relationship between various facets of communication and measures of satisfaction. Thus, for example, job satisfaction has been shown to correlate significantly with frequency of communication with supervisors (Baird & Diebolt, 1976). It has also correlated with openness in communication between subordinate and supervisor (Burke & Wilcox, 1969). General satisfaction with communication is also important to job satisfaction (Downs, 1977; Roberts & O'Reilly, 1974a). Elsewhere, surveys of communication in 16 organizations involving close to 4000 employees indicated consistently strong relationships between communication and satisfaction. Across organizations, the most important contributor to job satisfaction was "organizational communication relationships" (explaining 50% of the variance). In particular, the quality of superior–subordinate relationships and the degree of involvement in the system were the most important of four factors used to characterize organizational communication relationships (Goldhaber et al., 1978).

While the correlations reported in these studies have all been in the positive direction, negative relationships for certain communication variables have also been noted. For example, too much communication can also be dissatisfying (Blau, 1954; Roberts & O'Reilly, 1974b, 1974c).

Other research linking various communication-related variables to different dimensions of job satisfaction has been reported, using the job descriptive index (which measures five aspects of job satisfaction) as well as the Minnesota satisfaction questionnaire (Roberts & O'Reilly, 1974a). For example, in a sample of 89 professional and nonprofessional employees in mental health care teams, accuracy of information received from supervisors was significantly related to satisfaction with work, promotion opportunities, satisfaction with supervision, and overall satisfaction. In addition, satisfaction with communication was significantly related to satisfaction with work, pay, supervision, and overall satisfaction. Similar results were also obtained in two samples of military personnel. The pattern of obtained results gives further support to the view that communication behavior and the antecedents are pertinent to relevant dimensions of job satisfaction.

Looking more directly at what constitutes satisfaction with communication per se, research suggests that this construct is multidimensional in nature. Among seven dimensions isolated by Downs and Hazen (1977) in six organizations, the most critical ones for job satisfaction were communication climate, personal feedback, and communication relationships with superiors.

COMMUNICATION AND PERFORMANCE

Another general area of concern involves communication and performance. Questions here pertain to how much and what kind of communication yield maximum performance. As for how much, Price (1968) argues that high levels of communication increase coordination within organiztions, which in turn enhances organizational effectiveness. He further suggests that greater amounts of instrumental communication are likely to lead to a lower rate of turnover (Price, 1977, p. 73). As for what kind, specifying the particular variables or components of communication and their specific impacts on productive behavior is not necessarily easily or directly noted (Porter & Roberts, 1976, p. 1565). Rather than directly influencing behavior, communications may affect the ways receivers organize their images of the environment, and this organization influences the way they behave (Roberts, 1971, p. 361). Elsewhere, Hawkins and Penley (1978) have proposed a model that suggests that communication affects motivation, which in turn influences employee performance. Initial exploratory research testing this expectancy model suggested that supervisor and top management communication were both important factors in affecting expectancies linking effort to performance and performance to rewards. The models we present in Chapters 2, 3, and 4 also propose a two-step approach, linking communication style of senders to outcomes in performance mediated by the senders' perceived credibility.

Hierarchical Effects. A number of studies have considered this relationship from different perspectives and levels of analysis. Within hierarchical organizations, for example, it has been noted that increased effective upward communication from lower to higher levels of management tends to increase decision-making quality (Lawrence & Lorsch, 1967) and perceived quality of decision implementation

(Pascal, 1978). Elsewhere, it has been noted that the free flow of information and communication is important to effectiveness in organizations that use normative sanctions and relatively low degrees of administrative control (e.g., general hospital organizations), whereas in organizations using coercive sanctions and high control (e.g., mental hospitals, prisons), restriction of information and high control may enhance organizational effectiveness (Julian, 1966). This in turn suggests a contingency view of managing communication and information flows depending on the goals, norms, and tasks of the hierarchical organization.

Group Effects. In work groups and among individual workers and their immediate supervisors, decision-making performance of subordinates has been shown to improve with frequency of interaction with superiors (O'Reilly, 1977). Objective measures of individual and group productivity have been positively correlated with ease and freedom of communication between superiors and subordinates (Indik, Georgopoulos, & Seashore, 1961). Elsewhere, Jain (1973) found positive relationships between supervisory communication and performance in urban hospital settings using perceptual measures of performance.

While these studies are generally supportive of a communication performance linkage, much research is needed to clarify this relationship further. In particular, proper identification of the relevant mediating variables and the specific context (nature of technology, task, etc.) within which communication occurs is needed in order for this linkage to be better understood.

Conclusion

This review of theoretical perspectives and empirical research, though not exhaustive, has attempted to capture major strands of current thinking and research on organizational communication. In a very broad sense, the literature referred to here suggests some basic guidance and direction for theory development and communication practice in an operational sense.

In terms of basic patterns, it seems evident that communication behavior does influence such attitudes as satisfaction with the communicator and to some extent broader areas of job satisfaction.

Thus, managers could well benefit from giving careful attention to what and how they communicate with subordinates, peers, and superiors. Moreover, there is sufficient evidence to suggest a relationship between communication and such behavioral outcomes as individual worker and group productivity. The particular mechanics and linkages in this relationship may not be direct, but at least an indirect relationship is evident.

These two general observations strongly suggest that managers at all levels need to think in terms of actively *managing* their communication and information environment in a way that facilitates positive employee attitudes and performance. Thus, encouraging the development of appropriate communication linkages within and across organizational boundaries becomes a major concern for enhancing organizational effectiveness. Determining the appropriate linkages and amount of communication is largely an art, but sensitivity to certain key contextual factors can provide clues in coping with this issue.

In this connection, perhaps the strongest message that emerges from the literature to date is the view that communication processes need to be analyzed and understood in the particular context within which they occur. Thus, what works or happens in one communication context may not necessarily work the same way in another context. The challenge for theorists and practitioners is to develop a framework for understanding which variables or factors are most critical and how they interact with communication processes.

As has been suggested earlier, theory building in this realm is in its beginning stages. What seems called for at this point is some "middle range" theory development (Merton, 1957), which in turn can contribute to broader, more encompassing theory over time. Some beginning steps in this direction are starting to appear, but much work remains. While work is going on at this level, there is also considerable room for the development of "practice theory" (Friedlander & Brown, 1974; Weisbord, 1976) that can provide practitioners with additional guidance in their day-to-day concerns for improving existing communication behavior within organizations.

In a tentative sense, our review of the literature suggests some bare bones attempts in this direction by initially specifying concern for context, content, and interpersonal relations. The literature review also will serve as the backdrop for assessing how communication content and processes relate to particular attitudinal and behavioral outcomes.

In Chapters 2, 3, and 4 we attempt to construct and test a model reflecting these elements and their interrelationships. In doing so, we will focus on the relationship between individual communication behavior and specific outcomes within organizational settings. Although not all-encompassing, our discussion identifies critical elements of communication behavior that can help to enhance attitudes and performance of one's colleagues.

2

The Impact Model

A structure will now be provided to link several constructs about communication into an integrated framework for understanding and describing the impact of an individual's communication behavior on other people who work with the individual. The model draws on previous writings and studies as well as on recent field research conducted by the authors. It provides a way of systematically exploring a person's communication behavior within an organizational context. Specific individual and organizational outcomes are included in the accounting. In the concluding portion of this chapter, a summary of the research strategy is outlined to test various aspects of the model.

Model Building

In the behavioral sciencies, models are developed in an effort to represent some portion of the real world and to identify particular variables and possible linkages among them in a way that clarifies, simplifies, and promotes understanding. Yet it is evident that "every model of a real system is in one sense second-rate. Nothing can exceed, or even equal, the truth and accuracy of the real system itself [Ashby,

1970, p. 40]." Thus, the model-building process has very obvious limits, particularly since it may oversimplify and miss critical components that should be included. Achieving a delicate balance between under-specification and overspecification is indeed difficult.

In the discussion that follows, the limits of model building are fully recognized. Nevertheless, the hope is that the proposed model may help to clarify and promote understanding as to how communication behavior affects individual and organizational life. In developing this model, we have proceeded from an extensive review of material on organizational communication, drawing on certain linkages proposed in other studies and in turn have integrated such work with our own in an effort to develop a more operational framework for examining specific aspects of communication style and its impact on colleagues in the work setting.

The Impact Model

Definitions

Focal person—the individual whose communication behavior is the center of concern.

Colleagues—those individuals who are in the focal person's communication net in his or her work environment. They can be subordinates, peers, superiors, clients, or customers of the focal person.

Communication style—a set of critical, essential elements or behaviors that in combination can be used to describe in a generalized way how a focal person communicates with colleagues.

Credibility—the extent to which colleagues regard a focal person as worthy as a source of information.

Outcomes—the satisfaction of colleagues with the focal person, job satisfaction, role clarity of colleagues, and colleague effectiveness (primarily that of subordinates) on the job.

Postulates

The general proposition that ties the model together is that a focal person's interpersonal communication style has an important impact on his or her colleagues' satisfaction with their jobs or roles and with the focal person. A focal person's style also influences colleagues' role clarity and effectiveness in their work.

This proposition should appear intuitively quite reasonable. Yet, research to support it systematically and empirically has been quite limited to date. Moreover, we postulate that the basic proposition is insufficient to explain the presumed linkages between a focal person's communication behavior on the one hand and colleague attitudes and behavior on the other. More specifically, the set of relationships shown in Figure 2.1 is suggested.

As can be seen, this model posits a set of causal linkages in which a focal person's communication style is seen to influence a colleague's perception of the focal person's credibility and that this perception, in turn, largely influences colleagues' attitudes and performance. Hence, we move beyond the direct communication–outcome conception to a two-stage model. The intervening factor of the credibility of the communicating focal person (in the opinion of the receiving colleague) is seen to act as a filter that determines the nature and extent of the effects of the focal person's communication style on his or her colleagues' attitudes, role clarity, and effectiveness.

Also indicated in the model is a feedback loop from colleagues' reactions to the subsequent communication behavior of the focal

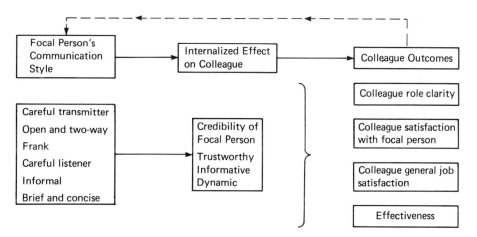

Figure 2.1. Initial model representing impact of focal person's communication style on colleagues.

person, indicating that the nature of colleague reactions may, to some extent, cause focal persons to modify the way they subsequently communicate to their colleagues. In turn, the extent to which such a feedback loop actually operates will depend on the focal person's sensitivity to signals he or she may pick up from colleagues' reactions to the initiating style of communication.

With these basic elements of the model presented generally so far, we turn now to a more detailed consideration of the three components and the rationale for the proposed linkages.

Communication Style—What Is It?

A few studies have indicated the importance of open, two-way communication as a specific measure of managerial interpersonal communication behavior (Argyris, 1962), but other specific dimensions of communication behavior have not been extensively probed. Schein (1969) described communication style as referring "to a whole range of things such as whether the person is assertive, questioning, pedantic, or humorous; whether his tone of voice is loud, soft, grating, or melodious; whether he accompanies his words with gestures, and so on [pp. 19–20]." Elsewhere Wofford et al. (1977) suggested that a communication style represents a "category of communication behaviors which have related purposes and similar approaches and [that] a particular style will be used with consistency by a person for similar situations [p. 148]." Thus, a person may choose to vary his or her style depending on the particular context but will generally employ a given style more or less consistently when similar situations arise.

Our own view of interpersonal communication style is generally consistent with these ideas. Yet, the concept of communication style has been employed and associated with a considerable range of behaviors.

We need to understand and to specify what behaviors are involved since it is these behaviors and the messages they convey that influence the attitudes and effectiveness of the recipients. The issue thus becomes one of identifying and making explicit what factors or components are most critical in characterizing a person's style of communicating.

Previous efforts in this direction have tended to identify one or two variables at a time (such as a person's frankness, openness, listening skills) for investigation, and only since the late 1970s have efforts been undertaken to examine more systematically the multidimensionality of communication style. Except in one or two instances, however, these studies have not addressed communication behavior in actual organizational work settings.

Thus, a central concern in our research is to take a careful look at identifying essential components of a person's communication behavior or style and then to examine the extent to which these factors in combination may help to explain or influence the credibility of a communicator in the eyes of other persons and have some effect on other people's attitudes and behavior. The task of identifying specific components of interpersonal communication style will be taken up in greater detail later in the chapter.

Importance of Credibility as a Mediating Factor

The next link in the model suggests a first-level outcome of interpersonal communication style—namely, the creation of an image of credibility of the communicator in the eyes of those receiving the communication. The theoretical and conceptual basis for suggesting communicator credibility as a critical intervening variable can be traced back to the fundamental set of communication research studies carried out in the early 1950s and discussed in a volume by Hovland, Janis, and Kelley (1953). The focus of this research was on persuasive communications and their effects on opinion change and behavior. A basic feature of that work was the notion that the weight or impact of a communicator's assertions on an audience or receiver will depend on both (a) the extent to which a communicator is perceived to be a source of valid assertions ("expertness") and (b) the degree of confidence in the communicator's intent to communicate the assertions he or she considers most valid ("trustworthiness") (Hovland et al., 1953, p. 21).

Since Hovland's seminal work, a number of other investigations have examined communicator credibility (often called "source credibility") and related notions of ethos and interpersonal trust.[1] Such studies have

---

[1]Specific studies and review articles that have looked at credibility and related concepts include Anderson and Clevinger (1963), Giffin (1967), Bowers and Phillips (1967), McCroskey (1966), Berlow, Lemert, and Mertz (1969), Fulton (1970), Falcione (1974a, 1974b), and Carbone (1975).

focused primarily on the credibility of public figures as perceived by undergraduate students. Only gradually have efforts been made to apply this concept of credibility to ongoing work organizations. Steps in this directions are reflected in studies where the effects of a generalized concept of interpersonal trust were examined in relation to the behavior of individuals, work groups, and the larger organization (Friedlander, 1970; Gibb, 1964; Read, 1962; Roberts and O'Reilly, 1974b, 1974c; Zand, 1972). More recently, however, attention has been given to specific components of credibility (safety, expertise, and dynamism) and their relationship to communication in work settings (Falcione, 1974b; O'Reilly & Roberts, 1976). In general, these dimensions of credibility have been found to be significantly related to satisfaction with supervision and key communication variables.

It should be noted that these studies do not directly test for a causal relationship; however, the general implication is that credibility is an initial precondition that influences the extent to which a communicator will be able to bring about intended changes in attitude and behavior on the part of receivers. Thus, credibility has generally been viewed in terms of having particular communication effects.

But where or how does a person (the intended receiver) develop a particular perception of another person's communication credibility in a work setting? A number of factors may contribute to this process, including the extent to which a focal person is viewed as a powerful person who can make things happen and influence his or her own superiors. As indicated in our model, however, we are proposing that it is the particular communication style of a person that largely determines how credible he or she is seen to be by colleagues. Thus, the communication behavior of a person shapes the image or perception others have of that person, and this perception in turn mediates the extent to which other persons will respond to the communication behavior and message content conveyed by a focal person.

This linkage from interpersonal communication style to credibility was suggested, for example, by Deutsch (1958), who found communication to be a central variable in the development of trust (a form of credibility) in a series of laboratory studies. However, he did not directly examine the specific kinds of communication behaviors that apply in an ongoing organizational setting. In a more general sense, however, the idea that credibility or trust is based on authentic, open communication has been consistently suggested in the organization development literature as a precursor to improved organizational effectiveness (Argyris, 1962; Likert, 1967).

Evidence of the linkage from focal person credibility as an information source and communicator on the one hand to colleague (primarily subordinate) outcomes on the other is suggested in the work of Gibb (1964), who found that lack of trust in information flow causes groups to operate at lower efficiency. In a longitudinal study, Friedlander (1970) found that trust facilitated group accomplishment, while Roberts and O'Reilly (1974c) found a positive relationship between trust in supervisor and subordinate job satisfaction. Elsewhere O'Reilly and Roberts (1976) reported a positive relationship between three aspects of supervisory credibility and subordinate perceptions of information accuracy. However, these studies have not directly examined credibility as a mediating factor as suggested in our model.

The idea of perceptions as a key element in the communication process is consistent with other discussions of communication in organizational settings (e.g., Haney, 1973; Huseman, Lahiff, & Hatfield, 1976). It recognizes that the communication process is interactive, involving not just the attributes and behavior of a sender but those of receivers as well. An approach of this nature also acknowledges that the perception process is influenced by many factors, not just the communication behavior of a sender, but our view is that interpersonal communication style plays a critical role in the development of particular perceptions of focal persons in the work setting.

Outcomes

The final link in our model points to the impact of communication behavior on receivers as mediated by the communicator's credibility. Here we are getting at the "so what?" question of communication. That is, what difference does the communication (as mediated by credibility) make in terms of attitudes, knowledge, and behavior of receivers?

In terms of attitudinal outcomes, prior research has suggested a consistent linkage between communication and satisfaction. In particular, individuals having good communication (*good* being defined in many different ways) with their bosses and other colleagues are generally more satisfied with those persons and with other facets of their job situtations. From our perspective, these general considerations are translated into two specific aspects of satisfaction as central outcomes of concern: satisfaction with communicator and general job satisfaction. Thus, we would argue that a person's general feeling and attitude toward a focal person communicator is considerably influenced by the nature and quality of communication from that focal person. The extent to which the focal peson uses a communication style that creates a credible image in the eyes of others will in turn increase satisfaction with that person. At a broader level, interpersonal communication from the focal person is also seen to influence a colleague's (particularly a subordinate's) general satisfaction with the job. This view is based on the idea that communication activity is so pervasive that the nature and quality of interaction with a focal person (assuming he or she is a central figure in the job situation) will have an important impact on general satisfaction with the job.

Apart from attitudinal impacts, changes in knowledge or understanding (stemming from the content of communications) are outcomes that also need to be considered. Central to changes in knowledge and understanding is the extent to which communication from the focal person helps to clarify the role and responsibilities of the colleague in question. This impact is rather obvious where the focal person is the supervisor of the colleague–receiver. It is this relationship that tends to receive the most attention. However, interaction among peers (the focal person interacting as a colleague with others at the same organizational level) may also influence an individual's sense of role clarity. This would seem to be especially important in a work group where the task performance depends on the individual's role clarity or where the tasks of individual members are highly interdependent.

The importance of role definition and role linkages among persons in an organization is rooted in previous theoretical work by Katz and Kahn (1966, 1978). They, in fact, characterize organizations as a systems of roles where people are tied together in terms of the functional interdependency of roles they assume. The concept of role in this context provides a means for linking the individual to the organization as a whole and to others within the organization. The process whereby individuals learn and assume organizational roles involves a number of steps in which possible discrepancies between the original expectations of the role sender and the actual role behavior of another person can occur. A key element in removing discrepancies would seem to be the communication that takes place between role sender and role receiver. This perspective on the relationship between role expectations and role behavior thus has direct relevance for the model proposed in our research strategy. Moreover, there is a fair amount of research that supports this role theoretic view and the linkage to communication behavior and organizational performance.[2]

An outcome of particular importance in the world of work is the extent to which a communication ultimately affects effectiveness of individuals in their work. For example, in a hierarchical relationship, colleagues who are subordinate to a focal person may be expected to accept directions from the focal person as to what they should do, how they should perform their tasks, and the priorities to be observed in completing the various tasks. In this instance, we are concerned with individual and work unit level effectiveness and the extent to which a focal person's communication behavior mediated by his or her credi-

---

[2]The importance and impact of role clarity (or its opposite—role ambiguity) on employee attitudes and behavior has been reported in several research studies. Kahn, Wolfe, Quinn, Snock, and Rosenthal (1964), for example, indicate that role ambiguity is a concern for a substantial percentage of our labor force. Although the causes of role ambiguity for an individual in an organization cannot be entirely attributed to any given focal manager, clearly a manager does have a primary responsibility to define for and with colleagues (particularly subordinates) specific job and role relationships. Recognition of this responsibility and relationship to supervisory performance is suggested in a survey conducted by Mandell (1956), who found that supervisors rated low in performance were also rated poorly for their ability to issue clear instructions to their subordinates. Elsewhere, Cohen (1959) has reported that ambiguous task definition was associated with a less favorable attitude toward the superior and decreased productivity. Smith (1957) has also found that increased role ambiguity leads to a decrease in problem solving efficiency. More recently, House and Rizzo (1972) have reported findings that suggest role clarity as an important intervening variable linking independent variables (organization formalization practices and leadership practices) with dependent variable measures of organizational effectiveness, employee satisfaction, anxiety–stress, and propensity to leave or stay. This particular study provides some tangential linkages to communication behavior, but it still does not directly measure specific dimensions of communication behavior that may affect role clarity and dependent measures of concern. Another study cited earlier (Indik, Georgopoulos, & Seashore, 1961) points to a direct link between open and two-way communication between superior and subordinate on the one hand and subordinate performance on the other. Increased role clarity would seem to provide a reasonable explanation for the relationship that was observed, although no measure of role clarity was included in the study. While these various studies do not directly test all the role clarity linkages proposed in our model, in combination they do lend support for the notion that role clarity can be an important outcome of managerial communication behavior.

bility will in turn influence the job-related behavior of others (primarily subordinates) in the work setting.

Conceptually this relationship between communication and behavior seems quite reasonable, though it is also obvious that other factors— such as company policy, special incentives, the individual employee's ability, and the quality of the equipment provided—will affect an individual's effectiveness. Thus, we anticipate that the impact of a focal person's communication on the effectivenss of individuals in performing their work will be less than its impact on satisfaction with the focal person as such.

Closing the Loop

The outcomes described in the preceding section in turn become the ingredients of future action that may entail feedback to the communicator as well as subsequent communication to others. That is, the receiver in turn also becomes a sender, triggering another cycle in the process. Thus, we incorporate into the model feedback and "feedforward" to underscore the dynamic nature of the communication—outcome process. The causal flow from style through credibility to particular outcomes must therefore be understood as a helical process (Dance, 1967), moving forward as it partially feeds back.

Assessing causality in a real-world context thus becomes a difficult task. Strictly speaking, one can argue that everything is mutually interactive in the realm of organizational behavior. We will focus more directly on the methodological implication of this issue in the next chapter. For the moment, our concern here is to point out and acknowledge the dynamic nature of the communication process and to reemphasize that no final end state (outcome) can be ultimately captured.

Operational Measures for Model Elements

In the discussion up to this point, we have proposed a model that posits a relationship between a focal person's communication behavior, an intervening factor (the focal person's credibility), and outcomes involving satisfaction with focal persons, general job satisfaction, role clarity, and effectiveness in the work setting. Operational measures for these factors have been derived from field research done by the authors as well as from other organizational behavior research.

Dimensions of Communication Style

In investigating what factors or behavioral components are at the core of interpersonal communication style, we proceeded in two phases. In Phase I, we identified a range of potential behaviors that might be related to interpersonal communication. In Phase II, we examined, refined, and isolated from this broad range of behaviors specific sets of behaviors that held promise for further investigation.

PHASE I: INTERVIEW ANALYSIS

We began with a series of individual interviews with managers from three divisions (manufacturing, research and development, and marketing) of a large information technology firm. The purpose was to identify specific behaviors that describe the different ways managers communicate with others. In these interviews, managers were asked to think of someone in the organization whom they considered to be a highly effective communicator and to identify the behaviors and characteristics that describe this person's style of communication. After describing the characteristic behaviors of highly effective communicators, interviewees were asked to describe behaviors of someone they considered to be a poor communicator. Behaviors relating both to sending as well as to receiving messages were identified as part of this process. In addition to these two sets of questions, the respondents were also asked if they noticed and could identify differences in effective communication, depending on whether it was upward, downward, or lateral. The consistent responses to this question was that no one behavior could be uniquely linked to a particular direction of communication.

Most interviews were tape-recorded, and where this was not possible, notes were taken during the course of the interview. From these conversations a series of statements were extracted that described behaviors of good and bad communicators as perceived by the interviewees. These statements were then reviewed, refined, and reduced to a set of 73 items that captured the range of behaviors that had been identified. Seven-point scales (ranging from "always" to "never") were attached to each item, using anchor words at each point shown to approximate equal intervals in ratio judgments of frequency (Bass, Cascio, & O'Connor, 1974). These items plus two questions about role effectiveness were combined into a questionnaire that was used in the second phase of the research.

PHASE II: QUESTIONNAIRE ANALYSIS

Phase II of the research involved the distribution of the questionnaire to over 700 managers in an industrial setting. Of the 719 questionnaires sent out, 397 usable responses were obtained (a 55% return rate). The responses were subjected to a factor analysis (principal factors with varimax rotation) that yielded six factors that were seen to be suitable for further investigation.

Each factor was analyzed by first identifying those items that had high loadings on that factor. A minimum factor loading cutoff point of .35 was used to initially isolate the key items on a factor, and the loadings of these items on other factors were in turn assessed to be sure that only items that had at least a .10 higher loading on that factor compared to other factors would be retained. The resulting set of items on a given factor was then studied in order to develop a term or phrase that seemed to give appropriate meaning to the construct represented by that set of items. In this manner, key items for each factor were identified and factors were labeled.

An analysis of Factor 1 revealed six items above the .35 cutoff, and four of these had factor loadings of more than .50. These items all focused on the idea of careful organization of thoughts and choice of words when communicating with others (e.g., chooses words carefully, organizes thoughts before speaking). Accordingly, this factor was labeled *careful transmitter* (see Table 2.1 for sample items).

Factor 2 contained 20 items with loadings of .35 or above, of which 13 loaded .50 or more on the factor. Looking at the items with highest factor loadings, the notion of an open, free flow of two-way communication (e.g., asking for other people's views, giving feedback) emerged very strongly, and thus this factor was labeled *open and two-way*.

In analyzing Factor 3, nine items were identified and six of these had factor loadings of .50 or more. The items pertained to frank, self-assured communicating style, and the factor was accordingly labeled *frank*.

TABLE 2.1
Dimensions of Communication Style (Factors Based on Factor Analysis and Sample Items from Colleague Questionnaire)

Factor	Sample items
1. Careful transmitter	He speaks deliberately when he communicates. He chooses his words carefully.
2. Open and two-way	He is receptive to points of view that differ from his. He follows up conversations with feedback.
3. Frank	He is frank in saying what he really thinks. He levels with others when he disagrees with their viewpoints.
4. Careful listener	He keeps his mind on what the speaker is saying. He lets me finish my point before he comments.
5. Informal	He is very informal and relaxed when he communicates. He is very natural in the way he relates to others.
6. Brief and concise[a]	His comments are brief and to the point. He takes a lot of words to say something that could be said in a very few words.

[a]As noted in Chapter 3, this scale dropped out in a subsequent factor analysis and was excluded from later analyses.

Factor 4 yielded eight items, of which three loaded .50 or more on the factor. The items related to communicator attentiveness and carefulness in listening to others. Thus, this factor was labeled *careful listener*.

Factor 5 included three key items, all of which focused on the notion of natural, relaxed informality in communicating with others (e.g., he's very informal and relaxed with others). Hence, this factor was called *informal*.

Nine items loaded heavily on Factor 6 (five had a .50 or more factor loading), and they consistently referred to the notion of conciseness (e.g., brief and to the point) or to the opposite notions of wordiness or lack of brevity (e.g., he tends to run off at the mouth), which had negative factor loadings. This factor was therefore labeled *brief and concise*.

SCALE RELIABILITY

Scales were developed based on these six factors, and the internal consistency reliability (coefficient alpha) was then calculated. As part of this process, items were dropped when they no longer contributed to increasing the scale reliability or when an alpha of .85 was reached for a scale. The items were also correlated with item total (factor) scores of the other factors, and where an item correlated higher with a factor score other than its own factor, it was dropped from that scale. This process yielded a set of 25 items for a shortened questionnaire instrument in which the six scales had reliabilities of .76 and above. An additional analysis to examine the retest reliability of these scales was generally quite satisfactory. The test–retest correlation coefficients for a sample of 36 respondents each describing a focal person (administered 1 week apart) ranged up to .85 for careful transmitter.[3]

RELEVANCE OF THE COMMUNICATION STYLE FACTORS

It should be noted that the factors that emerged from this research have turned up earlier in commentaries about effective communications. Factor 1, careful transmitter, is generally seen as a principle of effective speaking and points to the necessity of carefully organizing one's thoughts in order to transmit information to others. In this connection, Petrie (1963) has concluded on the basis of a review of existing literature that messages which are well organized lead to better comprehension and retention on the part of the receiver. He indicates, however, that there is surprisingly little direct research to substantiate this principle.

As mentioned earlier, open and two-way communication (Factor 2), has also been seen as important. Some small-group communication research, for example, indicates that an all-channel condition of communication in complex problem solving situations typically leads to better solutions (e.g., Bavelas, 1950; Shaw, 1964). Elsewhere, Burke (1969) has argued that "in order for speakers to be effective communicators, they need to receive some form of feedback from listeners." However, he cites no empirical support for this statement.

Factor 3, frank, fits with the literature on conflict management that stresses the value of surfacing differences and conflicting points of view in order to yield better decisions and solutions to organizational problems. The construct careful listener (Factor 4) is consistent with the concern expressed by Rogers and Roethlisberger (1952) and others

---

[3]Further discussion and detail concerning scale reliability is provided in Chapter 3 based on additional samples.

that empathetic listening is a key to effective interpersonal communication. The relationship of Factor 5, informal, to interpersonal communication effectiveness seems logical to the extent that informality increases a readiness to deal openly and honestly with others, although once again little direct research in this area has been reported. The effects of being brief and concise (Factor 6) have not been dealt with empirically to any great extent either, although intuition and articles on principles of effective speaking clearly suggest that brief, direct comments are much preferred to long-winded statements.

Credibility Dimensions

As indicated earlier, credibility can be viewed in terms of three separate dimensions, and the measures used here are derived from the factor analytic work of Berlo *et al.* (1969) as well as Falcione (1974b). The three dimensions are labeled here as *trustworthy*, *informative*, and *dynamic*. Trustworthiness refers to a sense of interpersonal safety that a person may feel toward another and gets at the extent to which a person is viewed as fair, pleasant, friendly, honest, just, and patient in dealings with others. In this sense, a person's credibility is in part a function of the extent to which others see him or her as an approachable, reasonable person who can be trusted and respected. Informativeness involves the extent to which a person is seen as well qualified, well informed, skilled, experienced, and well trained for a job situation. Thus, it gets at how knowledgeable and expert the person is about the work situation. The more knowledgeable and well informed the person is, the more credible he or she is in the eyes of others. Dynamism refers to the activeness of a person and includes such notions as how forceful, aggressive (versus meek), and energetic a person appears to be. In terms of the overarching notion of credibility, it suggests that a person must demonstrate a certain level of activity and energy (as opposed to being a silent and perhaps suspicious person) in relating to others in order for them to see the person as a credible referent point in a work environment.

A total of 20 items derived from Berlo *et al.* are employed to measure these three dimensions, and the items ask the respondents to indicate the extent to which the statements describe their own perspectives of the focal person. Sample items are shown in Table 2.2.

TABLE 2.2
Credibility Dimensions (Factors Based on Factor Analysis and Sample Items from
Colleague Questionnaire)

Factor	Sample items
Trustworthy	He is very just in his dealings on the job. He is very kind to me.
Informative	He is very authoritative concerning issues that arise at work. He is very well informed on issues concerning his areas of responsibility.
Dynamic	He is very forceful at work. He is very energetic in his job.

Outcome Dimensions

The first outcome measure focuses on colleague *satisfaction with the focal person*. The items for this scale are derived from a satisfaction with supervision scale with an internal consistency reliability coefficient of .89 (Bass & Valenzi, 1974). The measure of *general job satisfaction* is also based on the work of Bass and Valenzi (1974), and the internal consistency reliability of this scale is .90.

Role clarity is a construct that is derived from the work of Rizzo, House, and Lirtzman (1970). They employed the term *role ambiguity*, which we have rephrased in positive terms as *role clarity*. As originally defined, this concept was viewed "in terms of (1) the predictability of the outcome of responses to one's behavior and (2) the existence or clarity of behavioral requirement [pp. 155–156]." In developing their scale via factor analysis, however, Rizzo *et al.* found that the items hanging together most clearly were those concerned with the latter dimension. The internal consistency reliability of this scale is .80.

The final outcome measure focuses on the *effectiveness* of the individual work unit represented by the focal person and his or her immediate network. The specific measure used has an internal consistency scale reliability of .95 (Bass & Valenzi, 1974). Research (Solomon, 1975) indicates that this scale has reasonably high convergent validity with objective, independently gathered measures of performance. Sample items for each measure are shown in Table 2.3.

TABLE 2.3
Outcome Dimensions (Factors Based on Factor Analysis and Sample Items from
Colleague Questionnaire)

Factor	Sample items
Satisfaction with focal person	All in all, how satisfied are you with your focal person? In general, how satisfied are you that the way the focal person interacts with you is the right way for getting your job done?
Job satisfaction	All in all, how satisfied are you with your job? How satisfied are you that your own interests and abilities are being effectively used by the job you have?
Role clarity	I know what my own job responsibilities are. I know exactly what is expected of me in my job.
Effectiveness[a]	Compared to other units you have known, how do you rate the effectiveness of the unit supervised by the focal person? How effective is the unit supervised by the focal person?

[a]This scale was used in only one organizational setting (the information technology firm in Chapters 3 and 4), and thus results for this particular outcome are limited to that sample. The remaining three scales were used in all samples.

Research Strategy

In subsequent chapters, we examine this model in a series of analyses involving several sets of questionnaire data, all of which come from managers and their colleagues in a variety of organizations. The overall research strategy incorporates three features that have driven the entire effort:

1. A broad definition of colleague relationships to include not only subordinates and superiors of a focal person but also peers.
2. Practical application of the data that have been collected through feedback reports to those who have taken part in the research, wherever possible.
3. Collection of data from managers and their colleagues in a broad range of organizational contexts as a way of examining the general applicability of the model in different situations.

Broad Definition of Colleagues

The incorporation of peers and superiors as well as subordinates in our definition of the colleague group of a given focal person rests on the view that it is important to consider the effects of a focal person's communication behavior regardless of whether the role relationships are vertical (superior, subordinate) or horizontal (peer). In fact, as part of this research we will directly examine the extent to which role relationships may influence communication behavior and perceptions thereof. Thus, in some instances (e.g., Chapter 4), we will concentrate on focal person–immediate subordinate contexts, while in other instances (e.g., Chapters 5 and 9), we will consider variations in communication behavior and outcomes in a comparative sense based on organizational role relationship.

The general data collection procedure involved distributing questionnaire packets to focal persons, who in turn were asked to distribute up to 10 colleague questionnaires to those people they considered to be the key actors they communicate with at work. They were asked to include most if not all subordinates as well as their immediate superior. Colleagues completed the questionnaire in terms of how they saw the focal person as a communicator as well as other questions regarding the work setting. Focal persons completed a self-report questionnaire that asked them to describe themselves on the same dimensions. Thus, items illustrated in Tables 2.1, 2.2, and 2.3 were restated in the focal person questionnaire to have the focal persons respond to the same basic items as in the colleague questionnaire in rating themselves (see Appendixes A and B).

Practical consideration in data collection dictated that the specific colleagues included in the sample be chosen by the focal persons rather than through the usual random or total questionnaire approach. Randomized sampling procedures, while preferable in some respects, might suffer from the fact that colleagues could be included who really did not know the focal person well enough to rate them accurately. Also, response rates, typically, would probably be lower. It should be pointed out that for most middle managers, 10 colleagues normally constitute most if not all the key persons who know them well enough to rate them. If focal persons distributed only one or two questionnaires, we would expect a strong bias and restriction. If the mean number distributed is close to 10, then at least we can be confident that the focal persons were not a source of restriction sample. In almost every instance, data were in fact obtained from almost all the subordinates as well as superiors of each focal person.

Feedback Strategy

Feedback mechanisms were also incorporated into this data collection process. The process worked as follows. Each focal person received a precoded green questionnaire to be completed by the focal person and 10 precoded yellow questionnaires to be filled out by colleagues (subordinates, peers, and supervisor). Every questionnaire had a unique code number in the upper left corner. Instructions on the green questionnaire told the focal person to record the code numbers of the yellow questionnaires given to colleagues in the space provided on the cover page of the green questionnaire. (See Appendixes A and B for sample questionnaires.) Each colleague and focal person completed his or her questionnaire independently and then separately mailed the completed material in a preaddressed, stamped envelope to a central computer center for processing. This procedure protected the anonymity of colleague responses in that the system of unique code numbers allowed the anonymous matching of each colleague with his of her focal person by number rather than by name. The colleagues were further assured that the focal persons would not receive direct feedback of each colleague's responses but rather that the responses of all the focal person's colleagues would be combined into average scores that would be made available to the focal person only if more than three colleagues participated in the survey. Focal persons were also told that their own printed feedback forms would be returned for their eyes only.

These feedback forms were called *communication audits*, and the procedure enabled focal persons to compare how others saw them in a general way with their own self-ratings. Scale scores were derived for each dimension in the communication model by combining responses to all questionnaire items that formed a particular scale. (Responses to negatively worded items were transformed to enable addition to the positively worded items on a scale.) The number of items that made up each scale varied, thus yielding different ranges for scale scores. In order to simplify interpretation for participants, the total scores on each scale were therefore transformed to range from 1 to 9. This was accomplished for scales with 7-point scaled items by dividing the total score obtained from adding responses across all items by the number of items forming that scale. This value was then multiplied by 1.42871, and then .75 was subtracted so that it became a number ranging from 1.00 to 9.00. This number was then rounded on the communication audit sheet to a single digit ranging from 1 to 9. Some of the outcome dimensions were derived from 5-point scaled items. For a score derived from these items, the item total for the scale was divided by the number of items in that scale. This value was then multiplied by 2 and then 1 was subtracted. The resulting value was in turn rounded to range from 1 to 9. (A further discussion of how the scales were originally developed is provided in Chapter 3.)

For all measures, low scores (e.g., 1, 2, 3) would be scaled to reflect a low amount or degree and high scores (e.g., 7, 8, 9) would mean a high degree or amount on that measure or factor. A 4, 5, or 6 would be neither high nor low on a factor. In most instances, the communication audits were mailed back to focal persons along with a brief inter- pretation of terms. In other selected instances, the printed audits were also discussed with a researcher in small group training sessions of 2–3 hours to review the pattern of results and implications. (See Chapter 9 for a further discussion of the feedback process and communication audit format.) The promise of feedback in a nonthreatening context where immediate supervisors or individual subordinates or peers would not have access to the data provided additional impetus for participants to cooperate in the research.

This basic strategy was carried out for every sample with two exceptions, the initial sample that provided the data analyzed in the present chapter and the information technology firm discussed in the next chapter. In both these instances, only subordinate responses were collected. That is, a randomly selected individual would be asked to describe his or her own immediate superior (focal person).

The application of the feedback principle not only provided an incentive to participate but also offered some concrete information that could be used in the day-to-day work of focal persons who were sensitive to the value of effective communication behavior. This approach and emphasis on providing feedback has similarity to other research procedures, such as the use of communicograms in terms of the emphasis given to feedback, and reflects increasing concern with a training–feedback dimension to research in communication (Weinshall, 1979).

Sampling Diverse Organizations

Apart from this feedback strategy, another aim of our overall research effort was to access data in a number of different organizational settings as a way of testing the generalizability of the model. Samples were gathered from three large manufacturing firms, a civilian Navy support agency, military personnel in two different installations, and managers in several county level social service agencies. Hence, there was considerable variation in organizational mission, size, and background of personnel included in the research.

A brief summary by chapter of organization type, type of analysis, and type of feedback provided is shown in Table 2.4. It should be noted that in certain instances the same sample will be treated in more than one chapter because the nature or focus of analysis differs. Thus, in Chapter 3, for example, we treat methodological issues pertaining to the measures employed in our research and in Chapter 4 go on to the hypotheses suggested by the model.

Although the field-oriented research strategy we have pursued imposes some methodological constraints and limitations (discussed in the next chapter), the collection of data from managers and their colleagues in a variety of different organizational settings is in our view a major advantage.

Summary

This chapter has reviewed the basic rationale and initial research phases leading to the development of the communication impact model (summarized in Figure 2.1). The general predictions of the initial model in turn suggest a set of relationships that can be formulated into specific propositions that shape the research and guide the rest of the book. These propositions are stated as follows:

1. A focal person's communication style as defined in this chapter will to a large extent shape that person's credibility image in the minds of those with whom he or she regularly communicates.

2. This credibility image (as measured by trustworthiness, informativeness, and dynamism) will act as a mediating or filtering

TABLE 2.4
Summary of Research Strategy in Different Organizations

Chapter	Organization sample	Focus of analysis	Feedback provided
2	Information technology manufacturing firm; sample of managers from all levels of management	Questionnaire–scale development (subordinate colleague data)	No
3	Information technology manufacturing firm; sample of managers from three divisions (manufacturing; marketing; R&D)	Test of model components by factor analysis; scale reliability; validity issues (subordinate colleague data formed basis of analysis)	No
	Navy civilian agency; managers in a variety of functions	Test of model components by factor analysis; scale reliability; validity issues (subordinate colleague data formed basis of analysis)	Yes (mailed only)
	County social service agencies; managers responsible for social welfare program delivery	Test of model components by factor analysis; scale reliability; validity issues (subordinate colleague data formed basis of analysis)	Yes (in training session)
4	Same organizations as in Chapter 3	Test of model hypotheses (subordinate colleague data)[a]	(See above)
5	Navy civilian agency; social service agency reported in Chapters 3 and 4; diversified manufacturing firm (same as in Chapter 6); Military officers from two bases (same as in Chapter 7)	Context and content of communication (data from superiors, peers, and subordinate colleagues)	(See above)

6	Diversified manufacturing firm. Two groups of managers: high technology and traditional technology	Impact of organization size and technology on communication (data from subordinate colleagues)	Yes (mailed only)
7	Military officers from two bases; county social service managers (different from social service sample in Chapter 3)	Work–information environment: impact on communication (subordinate colleague data)	Yes (mailed to military officers; training session for social service managers)
8	Military sample from Chapter 7; industrial managers from Chapter 6 plus additional sample of managers from another firm. County social service managers (different sample from those reported in previous chapter)	Relation of leadership behavior to communication behavior; relation to managerial success (data from superiors, peers, and subordinate colleagues)	(See above, Chapters 6 and 7)
9	Navy civilian agency and county social service agency samples discussed in Chapter 3, and diversified manufacturing firm from Chapter 6. The military sample is the same one reported in Chapter 7	Focal person's versus colleague ratings of communication behavior (superior, peer, subordinate, and focal person data)	(See Chapters 3 and 6)
10	Social service sample (not reported elsewhere in book)	Leniency analysis	Yes (communication audit discussed in training session)

[a]For the outcome measures in the model, effectiveness data were collected only for the information technology firm. Information on the other three outcome variables was available for all three organizations.

mechanism in determining the following particular communication outcomes: satisfaction with communicator, general job satisfaction, role clarity, and colleague effectiveness.

3. The relative effectiveness of a particular communication style will vary somewhat across communication settings depending on such issues as the nature of the task, technology, persons involved, and related contextual factors.

Several clarifications to these general propositions need to be added, however. First, we would expect that the predictive power of the model will be stronger for some of the outcomes than for others. Specifically, we anticipate that the model will best predict satisfaction with focal person. This is based on the view that the nature and quality of interpersonal communication is the most direct and immediate mechanism whereby people establish positive or negative feelings toward other people.

Correspondingly, we would expect somewhat less strong predictive power for general job satisfaction. As has been pointed out elsewhere, job satisfaction is a multifaceted phenomenon incorporating a number of factors that contribute to employee feelings and attitudes toward the job (e.g., Smith, Kendall, & Hulin, 1969). We would expect the communication impact on this outcome to be most relevant for subordinates of focal persons (as compared to peers or superiors), since in most organizations the traditional superior–subordinate relationship still dominates individual employee activities and orientations to the job. In a like manner, we would expect role clarity to be best predicted for subordinates of focal persons (as compared to peers and superiors), recognizing, however, that other factors (nature of job, prior experience, etc.) also contribute to role clarity.

Finally, effectiveness in job performance is also expected to be significantly predicted by the model, but perhaps least adequately in relation to the other outcomes since other elements in the work environment (such as technology and skill level) directly and indirectly affect performance at the individual and work unit level. Focal person communication would be expected to have its greatest impact on subordinate colleagues rather than on peers and superiors.

3

Measuring Communication
and Its Impact

The communication model has been presented with a rationale linking various components of the model together. We now turn to methodological issues and initial data analysis pertaining to the model. First, we will consider the general question of causal inference as it relates to examining causal linkages in our two-stage model. Second, we will examine the reliability and validity of the measures used to test the model. Additional methodological considerations regarding the scales and statistical analyses performed in testing the model will be considered in the following chapter.

Causality

As outlined in Chapter 2, the general model guiding this research proposes a set of cause–effect relationships. A focal person's communication behavior is presumed to "cause" other people in that person's interpersonal communication network to form certain attitudes toward the focal person, and the job setting, as well as to influence their behavior on the job. This perspective raises several important theoretical as well as operational issues surrounding causal-inference thinking. These need to be addressed before proceeding to specification of hypotheses, data collection, analysis, and interpretation.

At an intuitive level, the notion of causality is quite straightforward. In our day-to-day life, we experience events in a way that suggests to us a causal interpretation for understanding relationships in the real world. For example, at a physiological level, we sense a cause–effect relationship when our hunger is reduced or eliminated after eating a solid meal. However, at a more complex psychological level as we begin to abstract from our experienced reality, cause–effect relationships are increasingly subjective and difficult to measure in an unbiased, objective, meaningful way.

It may be in principle possible to develop a conceptually tight causal model, but to provide incontestable evidence in support of it is another matter. We fully recognize the difficulties of developing and attempting to test a causal model in this research. Nevertheless, thinking in causal terms can help to increase understanding and in turn may assist in improving simplified models of reality. As Blalock has observed: "One admits that causal thinking belongs completely on the theoretical level and that causal laws can never be demonstrated empirically. But this does not mean that it is not helpful to think causally and to develop causal models that have implications that are indirectly testable [Blalock, 1964, p. 6]."

Although we can never completely "prove" a cause–effect relationship in the social sciences, research designs can be developed that increase our confidence in being able to make such inferences. Controlled laboratory experimental designs with manipulation of independent variables come closest to achieving this ideal. However, even with a well-controlled and implemented experiment, there is still the problem of generalizing to individuals in complex ongoing real-world organizational contexts. The dynamics of the work setting may be very different from those of the laboratory context. The very precision of the laboratory experiment in social sciences makes us less confident that its conclusions can be generalized to the field (Meehl, 1967). This dilemma is especially pertinent for research on individuals and groups in organizational contexts.

Field Approach Favored

In contrast to laboratory experiments, field research comes closer to the reality of the ongoing organizational life but in the process is subject to considerable loss of experimental control. Hence, our ability to make strong causal inferences is much more threatened since other factors (not controlled for) may be operating in a way such that any "effects" that may have been noticed could be due to variables not measured or inadequately measured. Typically, in any social science research, we are faced with a number of trade-offs: experimental control, the capture of the basic real-world conditions in which a problem exists, the costs (time and money) in being able to carry through on a particular research design, as well as opportunity and feasibility.

In the research strategy that underlies the present set of studies, we have opted for a survey research approach, recognizing that experimental control will suffer. However, it is our view that the current state of knowledge about communication processes in organizations is as yet very limited. We are still wrestling with broad questions about what it is we should by trying to understand better. Even if we could achieve high fidelity of real-world conditions in a laboratory context, conclusions obtained, while possibly rigorous, would be narrow and restricted in generalizability. The cost of the effort and the current needs for more broad-based treatment favors survey research in field settings (Bass, 1974).

Caveat. In opting for this approach, we recognize from the start that our research design has considerable limitations. We will be attempting to make statements regarding the ability of our model to predict certain kinds of outcomes. As a means of obtaining greater control, we will measure certain additional variables not directly specified in the model but that prior research suggests may influence communication behavior and outcomes. In this sense, we can introduce a certain amount of control over "third" factors that might be indirectly involved (e.g., size of work groups, task environment, technology, personal attributes). Such statistical techniques as the introduction of dummy variables and partial correlation analysis facilitate this kind of control. Moving from prediction to causal inference is another matter, however. Since our data collection is cross-sectional in nature, we are severely constrained and at best will be able to make weak causal inferences from our data. Specific statistical procedures employed as part of this process will include stepwise multiple regression, partial correlation analysis, and path analytic techniques, but the results must be viewed in tentative terms for the time being until subsequent research can more thoroughly test the model through longitudinal studies. Thus in a general sense, we are only at the beginning stages of examining a theoretical model. Clearly, longitudinal efforts must follow, but what is learned in the cross-sectional beginning will contribute to a more efficient design in those more difficult longitudinal efforts.

Operational Methodological Issues

Apart from conceptual questions about inferring cause and effect, a number of operational methodological issues also require attention, such as the reliability and validity of our measures. In determining estimates for these, we will draw on data collected in three different organizations. The first organization is a large firm that manufactures information technology equipment. The respondents come from the manufacturing, marketing, as well as R&D divisions of the firm. The second organization is a Navy support agency made up largely of federal civilian employees located in a large urban area. The third organization is composed of a subset of rural and urban county social service agencies of a northeastern state. Thus, these organizations represent a range of both private sector as well as public sector organizational settings. It should be noted that the analyses reported in this chapter are based on subordinates' ratings of focal persons.

Sampling Procedures

In the information technology firm, 450 managers (randomly identified from mailing lists containing the names of approximately 975 managers from this firm) were asked in a letter from the researcher to take part in this study. The randomly selected managers were sent a questionnaire that included biographical items as well as the items pertaining to the communication model described in Chapter 2.

Participants were instructed to complete the communication items in terms of how they saw their own superiors. The remaining items pertained to their own sense of role clarity, job satisfaction, satisfaction with supervision, and work unit effectiveness. The organization's interoffice mailing systems was used to distribute the questionnaires, and completed responses were in turn mailed by participants to a central collection point in the organization where they were picked up by the researcher.

A follow-up procedure to the first mailing list was used to request people who did not complete the original questionnaire to do so. The system worked as follows: Each recipient of a questionnaire was asked to mail a postcard (enclosed with the questionnaire) to the researcher that indicated whether or not the questionnaire has been completed. Recipients could also state on the card whether or not they wanted to receive a copy of the survey results. A master mailing list was used so that the researcher could check names on the postcards against the list and then contact each person who did not reply to the original mailing to urge cooperation in the research. This process yielded 340 returned questionnaires (75% response rate), of which 325 were included in the present analysis.

In the other two organizations, a modified data collection procedure was employed. In both organizations, the focal persons were initially identified by the participating organizations and given a packet of materials that included a questionnaire in which respondents completed a set of items describing themselves and their work situations. The questionnaire also included a set of biographical variables concerning the focal person. In both organizations, over 90% of the focal persons agreed to participate in the study.

Following the procedure outlined in Chapter 2, these focal persons were also asked to distribute up to 10 questionnaires to subordinates, peers, and superiors in their immediate work situations, who in turn responded to the same basic set of items in terms of how they viewed the focal manager and the work situation. The completed questionnaires were sent through interoffice mail to a central collection point and then forwarded in batch to the data processing center for analysis. The colleague response rate in the Navy support agency was over 80% and in the social service agency approximately 75%. As indicated in Chapter 2, profile feedback in the form of communication audits was subsequently mailed back to focal person participants in the Navy support agency. Focal persons in the social service sample received their communication audit printouts in a training session where the scores were further processed in small group discussion sessions. (Appendixes A and B contain the questionnaires used.)

Sample Description

The general biographical characteristics of the respondents from each organization are summarized in Table 3.1. Compared to the information technology firm, the other two organizations had greater representation of women respondents and the focal persons tended to be younger. In the county social service sample, the bulk of the respondents fell into the "other" category of primary function and indicated activities related to social work. Across organizations, size of department also differed considerably. Education level of respondents, however, was quite similar in the three organizations. A median level of 16 years represents a high school education (12 years) plus 4 years of college level training. In the Navy support agency and social service sample, focal persons were also asked how many people reported directly to them. (Focal person data were not collected in the information technology firm.) The responses indicated that the county social service focal persons typically had more subordinates reporting to them than did focal persons in the Navy support agency.

Reliability

An initial concern in the use of any survey instrument is the reliability of the measures included in the instrument, that is, the extent to which the measures are consistent in measuring the constructs of concern. Related to this overall issue is the extent to which such measures exhibit similar reliability in different samples in various organizational settings.

In approaching this question, we have focused on two kinds of reliability: the internal consistency of each scale and the retest reliability of the scales. The former "tells us something of how closely the obtained score comes to the score the person would have made at this particular time if we had had a perfect instrument [Guilford, 1965, p. 452]." The latter addresses the extent to which a person would

TABLE 3.1
Summary Profile of Biographical and Organizational Variables

Variables	Information technology firm[a] Subordinates N = 325	Navy civilian agency Subordinates N = 179	Navy civilian agency Focal persons N = 75	Social service agency Subordinates N = 117	Social service agency Focal persons N = 26
Average age	40.2	33.0	38.0	34.0	38.0
Sex					
Percentage male	99.5	57.5	80.0	24.8	40.0
Percentage female	.5	42.5	20.0	75.2	60.0
Median education level (years of education)	16.5	15.6	16.7	16.0	16.4
Primary function of department or division (%)					
Production	14.1	2.3	4.0		
Purchasing	3.2	1.8	1.0		
R&D	13.5	2.3	4.0		
Logistics	7.2	12.9	31.0		
Engineering	17.8	15.8	19.0		
Finance/accounting	10.1	41.5	19.0	2.6	4.2
Other	33.9	23.3	22.0	97.4	95.8
Median number of people in department or division	120.0		30.0		10.5
Median number of people in work group	6.3		8.0		5.5
Median number of people reporting to focal person			2.0		7.5

[a]Only subordinate responses were collected for this organization.

repeatedly get the same score if the survey were taken at different points in time (assuming that the thing being measured has itself not changed during the interim).

Internal Consistency

The internal consistency reliability of each of the scales in the model was evaluated by calculating alpha reliability coefficients for the three organizations. The results are reported in Table 3.2. Most of the alpha coefficients were above .80, thus suggesting quite strong consistency in each sample.

Test–Retest Reliability

Table 3.2 also includes retest reliability results for the scales based on data collected from a group of 37 MBA students, some of whom had worked full time for a few years or more while others had worked on a part-time or short-term basis. They were not members of the industrial or public sector samples that form the basis of the rest of this discussion. They completed the questionnaire twice, one week apart, and were asked to describe a focal person they previously or currently were working under.

For the 37 graduate students, the retest correlation coefficients were all large and statistically significant. The stability of the measures ranged from a high of .92 for satisfaction with focal person to a low of .56 for dynamic. In general, we concluded that the variables demonstrated high internal consistency reliability and were quite stable over the time tested.

Validity

Validity focuses on the general question: Are we in fact measuring what we say (or think) we are measuring? How close is the measure we use to the unobtainable true measure of the concept of consequence? In other words, in a very general sense, a measuring instrument is valid if it does what it is intended to do (Nunnally, 1967, p. 75). Validity is a

TABLE 3.2
Reliability Analyses[a]

	Alpha coefficients of internal consistency			Test–retest correlations[b] ($N = 37$)
Scale	Information technology firm ($N = 325$)	Navy support agency ($N = 179$)	Social service agency ($N = 117$)	
Communication style				
Careful transmitter	.81	.78	.70	.76
Open and two-way	.81	.78	.82	.82
Frank	.80	.63	.73	.85
Informal	.82	.75	.69	.88
Careful listener	.86	.86	.83	.89
Credibility				
Trustworthy	.90	.90	.91	.76
Informative	.93	.95	.93	.71
Dynamic	.85	.82	.77	.56
Outcomes				
Colleague-role clarity	.86	.85	.85	.64
Colleague/job satisfaction	.89	.92	.90	.68
Colleague satisfaction with focal person	.85	.85	.85	.92

[a]All analyses are based on subordinate ratings of focal persons who were their superiors.
[b]All coefficients are significant at $p < .001$ or better.

matter of degree, and it is a question of continuing concern to a researcher and practitioner, especially as one begins to apply an instrument across different types of settings and with different groups of people.

Two types of validity analysis were performed on the measures employed in our model. The first analysis considers what might be called the factorial validity of the scales. At issue here was the extent to which the factor structure of the scales was stable across samples. A high stability of structure would suggest that the scales are measuring a consistent set of constructs that have broader applicability than to just a single sample of persons from which the scales were originally developed. Such a pattern would suggest that we are getting a fairly generic set of constructs that have general meaning to people in a wide set of circumstances.

Factorial Validity

A factor analysis of the items included in the instrument was performed for each organization. The individual questionnaire items used to form the scales for each sample were blindly factor analyzed by the principal components method with varimax rotation to determine the consistency of the factor structure across different samples. We looked at whether the same structure appeared as we systematically changed various external parameters. If we found the same clustering repeatedly, we assumed that we were close to some true underlying invariant structure. In performing these analyses, the items were grouped into three separate panels for consideration. Thus, the communication style variables (colleague description of focal person communication behavior) were treated as one domain for a factor analysis. The credibility variables (how colleagues interpret the credibility of the focal person) were treated in a second factor analysis, while role clarity together with the remaining measures of satisfaction and effectiveness were grouped together for a third factor analysis.

FACTOR STRUCTURE IN COMMUNICATION STYLE

For two of the three organizations, a strongly consistent five-factor solution emerged, while the third (the social service sample) yielded a seven-factor solution. However, the two additional factors found in the social service agency setting were not stable or readily interpretable.

Overall, we concluded that underneath lay a consistent pattern of five components of communication style, as opposed to the originally derived six factors outlined in the initial model depicted in Chapter 2 (see Figure 3.1). The major difference between the original six factors and the factor obtained in the present analysis was that the items contained in "brief and concise" were partially absorbed by "careful listener" in the present analysis, or otherwise did not load consistently. The resulting five-factor solution for the communication scales is presented in Table 3.3, and this set of factors was accordingly employed in subsequent analyses of the model throughout the remainder of the book.

FACTOR STRUCTURE: CREDIBILITY

The factor analysis for the three credibility measures is strongly consistent across the three organizations and fits with previously obtained results reported in other research (Falcione, 1974b). The results are shown in Table 3.4.

FACTOR STRUCTURE: OUTCOMES

The third factor analysis dealing with role clarity, satisfaction, and effectiveness yielded a three-factor solution that was also very consistent for two of the three organizations. In the third organization, the

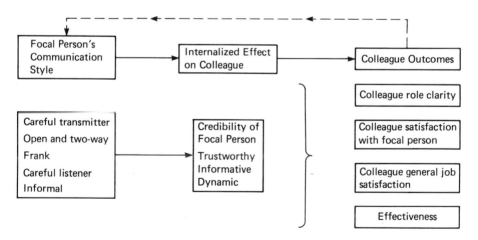

Figure 3.1. Revised model representing impact of focal person's communication style on colleagues.

TABLE 3.3
Factor Analysis of Communication Style Variables for Three Organizations[a,b]

Items	Careful listener A	B	C	Frank A	B	C	Informal A	B	C	Careful transmitter A	B	C	Open and two-way A	B	C	Communality A	B	C
Careful listener																		
1. Interrupts speaker	-.68	-.80	-.51													.62	.69	.69
3. Dominates discussions	-.71	-.72	-.50													.60	.54	.54
6. Keeps mind on speaker	.40	.50	.07								.45					.55	.68	.72
14. Jumps to conclusions	-.47	-.72	-.50									.41				.42	.70	.61
17. Runs off at the mouth	-.82	-.55	-.76								.43					.70	.57	.69
22. Lets others finish a point	.55	.67	.32												.56	.56	.67	.63
Frank																		
9. Says what he thinks				.62	.69	.61										.56	.61	.60
18. Does not mince words				.71	.48	.50										.55	.28	.36
21. Conveys self-assurance				.55	.16	.61					.57					.49	.38	.56
23. Levels with others				.57	.25	.76									.46	.49	.41	.72

	A[b]			B[b]			C[b]		
Informal									
7. Informal, relaxed when talking	.41			.63	.28	.42	.52	.45	.38
15. Relates naturally	.45			.76	.26	.75	.73	.57	.80
Careful transmitter									
2. Speaks deliberately		.42		.53	.53	.31	.51	.45	.36
4. Chooses words carefully				.81	.71	.76	.70	.66	.65
8. Organizes thoughts				.68	.62	.77	.67	.67	.70
11. Polished choice of words		.42		.62	.63	.45	.49	.53	.50
Open and two-way									
5. Asks others' views			.43	.51	.53	.62	.49	.34	.60
12. Seeks out information				.51	.46	.56	.39	.51	.61
13. Follows up with feedback			.45	.62	.66	.76	.49	.55	.63
16. Gives feedback				.60	.66	.77	.57	.54	.69
19. Receptive to different views				.51	.46	.24	.61	.50	.55

[a] Analysis is based on subordinate ratings of focal persons. Only factor loadings above .40 are reported.

[b] A = information technology firm; B = Navy civilian agency; C = social service agency.

TABLE 3.4
Factor Analysis of Credibility Variables for Three Organizations[a, b]

Items	Informative			Trustworthy			Dynamic			Communality		
	A	B	C	A	B	C	A	B	C	A	B	C
Informative												
27. Well trained	.83	.72	.75					.48		.80	.82	.74
30. Well qualified	.87	.79	.75							.84	.86	.75
35. Well informed	.57	.63	.75					.46		.52	.69	.74
39. Revelant	.78	.72	.72							.66	.66	.75
experience	.75	.83	.81							.77	.85	.84
48. Highly skilled												
Trustworthy												
26. Congenial				.78	.75	.80				.60	.69	.77
34. Friendly				.85	.83	.86				.72	.71	.79
38. Pleasant				.86	.88	.75				.75	.81	.78
Dynamic												
29. Aggressive							.82	.78	.65	.64	.55	.61
33. Hesitant							.52	.52	.02	.50	.52	.72
37. Energetic							.76	.77	.27	.61	.77	.78
40. Timid							.54	.34	.24	.51	.40	.75
47. Forceful							.66	.37	.46	.48	.18	.48
49. Active							.73	.66	.04	.60	.77	.74

[a]Analysis is based on subordinate ratings of focal persons in each organization.
[b]A = information technology firm; B = Navy civilian agency; C = social service agency.

information technology firm, some additional questionnaire items related to work unit effectiveness were included, which in turn yielded the additional factor for that organization. The results are shown in Table 3.5.

FACTOR CONGRUENCE

A subsequent analysis of the degree of factorial stability of the solutions across organizations is shown in Table 3.6. In this analysis, the solutions of the Navy and social service organizations were compared to those of the information technology firm. As can be seen, the congruency coefficients were for the most part very high, thus providing further evidence of the congruence of factor structures.

On the whole, these analyses provide strong support for the factorial consistency of the scales employed in our model and strengthen our confidence of their general applicability across different organizational settings.

TABLE 3.5

Factor Analysis of Outcomes Variables for Three Organizations[a, b]

Items	Role clarity A	B	C	Job satisfaction A	B	C	Satisfaction with focal person A	B	C	Effectiveness A	B	C	Communality A	B	C
Role clarity															
28. Knows job responsibility	.71	.77	.77										.59	.59	.61
32. Clear definition of authority	.66	.50	.58										.58	.31	.47
36. Knows what to do	.65	.50	.43					.45	.60				.63	.47	.61
42. Knows what is expected	.81	.88	.63						.57				.79	.84	.76
43. Divides time properly	.47	.65	.59										.26	.46	.35
51. Have clear goals	.58	.67	.48			.47			.45				.47	.63	.57
Job satisfaction															
56. Satisfied with organization				.55	.65	.66									
57. How satisfied with job				.73	.70	.75									
58. How satisfied about job future				.64	.75	.73									
59. Satisfaction with use of skills				.72	.82	.72									
60. Satisfaction with job progress				.60	.70	.63									
Satisfaction with focal person															
54. FP's skill in meeting people's needs							.66	.80	.74				.68	.67	.65
55. FP's ability to meet organization's needs							.58	.77	.49				.58	.61	.30
61. Overall satisfaction with FP				.41			.74	.81	.78				.82	.73	.64
62. Satisfactory relations with FP							.79	.77	.77				.80	.67	.67
Effectiveness															
51. Overall effectiveness										.80			.73		
52. Effectiveness compared to others										.69			.62		
63. Effectiveness improvement needed										.60			.49		

[a]Analysis is based on subordinate ratings of focal persons in each organization.

[b]A = information technology firm; B = Navy civilian agency; c = social service agency.

TABLE 3.6
Congruency Coefficient Analysis across Three Organizations[a]

Organizations[b]	Careful listener	Frank	Informal	Careful transmitter	Open and two-way	Trustworthy	Informative	Dynamic	Role clarity	Satisfaction with focal person	Job satisfaction
A with B	.90	.75	.50	.94	.98	.97	.95	.95	.99	.98	.96
A with C	.91	.94	.88	.85	.89	.98	.95	.82	.95	.94	.97

[a]See Harman (1967, p. 270) for statistical procedure employed.
[b]A = information technology firm; B = Navy civilian agency; C = social service agency.

Between versus "within" Focal Person Variances (Convergent Validity)

A second type of validity analysis was also performed on the data to get the extent to which the questionnaire items appear to discriminate between individual focal persons (as opposed to acting as a global representation of individuals in general). Put another way, we wanted to know if colleagues in describing their focal persons were actually describing discriminable environments or merely projecting their own needs, preferences, biases, or generalized views of interpersonal communication and outcomes. In completing the questionnaire, if each colleague was saying more about himself, herself, or people in general than about relationships to the individual focal person in question, then we should have observed more variance between colleagues describing a given focal person than between colleagues in different situations. Hence, we refer to this type of between versus "within" focal person variance as a form of convergent validity analysis.

To the extent we actually observed more variance in responses between colleagues vis-à-vis different focal persons than between colleagues within a particular focal person group, the more we could infer they were saying something specific and characteristic of the focal person rather than merely projecting their own biases or generalized views. There is, of course, another potentially plausible explanation for potential within-group homogeneity—namely, occupational similarities, selection, and norm formation. Nevertheless, it seems less plausible to attribute all greater within-group homogeneity in describing specific focal persons to such effects.

To test the extent to which colleague groups converged in their ratings of their focal persons, a simple one-way analysis of variance was performed for each organization sample on the scales included in the model. For each measure, the variance between focal persons as rated by their colleagues on the average was compared with the variance "within" focal persons as seen in the ratings obtained from colleagues rating the same focal person. Eta coefficients, F ratios, and their significance were computed (see Table 3.7). A significant variance between groups would indicate that the colleague groups were describing characteristics that they attributed to their own focal person rather than responding randomly or to general beliefs or biases about managers in general. The greater the F ratio and its significance and the larger the eta coefficient, which varies from 0 to 1, the greater the convergent validity as inferred from this analysis.

TABLE 3.7
Validity Analysis Based on Eta Coefficient[a]

	Eta coefficient		F ratio	
Scales	Navy civilian agency $N=179$	Social service agency $N=117$	Navy civilian agency	Social service agency
Communication style				
Careful listener	.80	.62	2.64**	1.94*
Frank	.64	.47	.94	.90
Informal	.63	.70	1.00	2.98**
Careful transmitter	.69	.60	1.20	1.79*
Open and two-way	.66	.65	.99	2.25**
Credibility				
Trustworthy	.70	.71	1.46	3.21**
Informative	.60	.60	.86	1.80*
Dynamic	.61	.59	.97	1.94*
Outcomes				
Role clarity	.52	.37	.61	.58
Satisfaction with focal person	.58	.48	.84	1.09
Job statisfaction	.49	.49	.53	1.17

[a]This analysis was not performed for the information technology firm since the sampling procedure in that organization involved only one subordinate description for each focal person. The number of groups on which the analysis is based for the other organizations is: Navy civilian agency = 33 groups; social service sample = 25 groups.
*$p < .05$
**$p < .01$

An examination of the eta values indicates similar patterns across samples for the most part. Most of the etas for the communication variables were reasonably high. The range was from .47 to .80, with most between .60 and .70. Etas for the three intervening variables measuring credibility were also relatively high, ranging from .59 to .71. For the consequence factors, the etas were generally lower across the board, particularly for the social service sample. Looking at the three factors in this category, satisfaction with focal person yielded a slightly higher eta than job statisfaction and role clarity. But this pattern is consistent with an interpretation that job satisfaction and role clarity are highly individualistic and actually more specific to the colleague respondent, whereas the other factor pertains more directly to the communication behavior of the focal person in question.

In sum, the convergent validity for 9 of 11 of these scales was seen to be quite strongly supported by the analyses.

Additional Methodological Issues

One issue that frequently occurs in looking at results in any analysis is whether or not other factors not being measured may actually provide a better explanation of results obtained. Thus, for example, it may be that size of work unit, physical proximity of focal person and colleague, or technology are more critical in explaining such outcomes as role clarity, effectiveness, or satisfaction than is interpersonal communication style. We will consider some of these alternatives in Chapters 6 and 7 for those organizations where such supplemental data are available.

Other methodological issues concern the assumptions associated with the nature of the data and the statistical procedures employed. One such issue involves the characteristics of the scales and the "desirable" direction of these scales. The issue of which direction is desirable for each scale is largely an empirical one that will be clarified by the data. There is, however, prior research discussed in Chapter 1 that indicates that colleagues do generally prefer the so-called desirable end of the continuum on the kinds of variables treated here. Thus, for example, people tend to prefer that a communicator be more of a careful listener, be more skilled as a careful presenter, encourage more two-way communication, etc.

With regard to the nature of the scales, it was pointed out earlier that they are multi-item measures and that a scale score thus represents responses to several individual scale items. As with other kinds of research in the field of organizational behavior, we will be treating such scales as interval in nature. It is recognized that the debates as to whether these kinds of multi-item scales should be considered interval has not been resolved in the literature (e.g., Nunnally, 1967; Rozeboom, 1966). However, as long as one can assume a monotonic relationship between an ordinal measuring scale and the underlying psychological scale, parametric estimates have been shown to yield few aberrations (Boyle, 1970; Labovitz, 1967, 1970). In the case of the scales employed in this research, anchor words were attached to each point on the scale shown to approximate equal intervals in ratio judgments of frequency and agreement (Bass *et al.*, 1974), which further strengthens our assumption of the monotonic nature of these scales. Hence, the position taken in this research is that these scales can be treated as interval for purposes of our analyses and that a possible violation of this assumption should not seriously jeopardize the interpretation of the data (recognizing, of course, the overall limitations on any type of research of this sort).

Given that regression analysis is the primary form of analysis employed here, we need to be sensitive to possible violations of the assumptions of normality, linearity, and homgeneity of variance. With regard to the normal distribution assumption, in all the samples under consideration in this research, our N sizes are quite large and thus possible violations should not cause a serious problem (Hays, 1963; Johnston 1963). In considering the assumptions of linearity and homogeneity of variance, examination of residuals and scatter plots indicates that the data did satisfy these requirements.

Mention should also be made of the moderate intercorrelation between some of the communication style variables. As can be seen in the correlation matrices for each sample (Tables 3.8, 3.9, 3.10), the correlation coefficients were typically in the .30–.60 range. While these levels do not suggest a severe multicollinearity problem, care should be taken in interpreting the relative importance of each independent variable, since regression coefficients are more likely to fluctuate somewhat across samples under these conditions. Also shown in these tables are the means and standard deviations of subordinates' responses on each scale. As noted in Chapter 2, each scale has a possible range of 1–9, with the higher numbers indicating a high degree of the characteristic or measure.

Summary

This chapter has treated a number of general methodological concerns related to the measures employed in our research. On the whole, the analyses reported here provide considerable support for the reliability, validity, and stability of the scales across a set of organizational contexts including both private and public sector organizations. The general consistency of results suggest that the measures included in our

TABLE 3.8

Subordinates' Means, Standard Deviations (*SD*), and Correlations for Information Technology Firm (*N* = 325)[a]

Scale	Mean	SD	2	3	4	5	6	7	8	9	10	11	12
Communication Style													
1. Careful transmitter	5.8	1.5	43	41	50	23	20	47	22	33	44	18	20
2. Open and two-way	5.7	1.5		51	52	57	57	58	34	58	74	48	39
3. Frank	6.3	1.6			29	43	20	53	57	38	53	26	25
4. Careful listener	6.5	1.4				42	39	42	-03*	37	51	31	29
5. Informal	6.0	1.9					37	46	19	44	61	33	31
Credibility													
6. Trustworthy	6.5	1.9						42	07*	46	58	41	32
7. Informative	6.8	1.7							50	53	77	48	41
8. Dynamic	7.3	1.4								27	42	24	17
Outcomes													
9. Role Clarity	6.5	1.5									62	48	48
10. Satisfaction with focal person	5.9	1.8										60	54
11. Job satisfaction	5.9	1.4											51
12. Effectiveness	5.9	1.9											

[a]All coefficients are significant at *p* < .01 except those with an asterisk. As noted in Chapter 2, the potential range of mean scores is from 1 to 9.

TABLE 3.9
Subordinates' Means, Standard Deviations (*SD*), and Correlations for Navy Civilian Agency (*N* = 179)[a]

Scale	Mean	SD	2	3	4	5	6	7	8	9	10	11
Communication Style												
1. Careful transmitter	6.5	1.6	57	50	57	51	46	53	36	49	60	30
2. Open and two-way	6.0	1.7		51	51	57	57	58	37	48	67	30
3. Frank	6.4	1.5			31	46	30	58	58	49	58	34
4. Careful listener	7.3	1.5				57	54	47	18	38	62	21
5. Informal	6.8	1.9					65	52	38	39	66	23
Credibility												
6. Trustworthy	7.5	1.6						48	32	47	66	27
7. Informative	7.6	1.8							63	42	78	25
8. Dynamic	7.1	1.4								42	56	23
Outcomes												
9. Role clarity	7.4	1.4									47	46
10. Satisfaction with focal person	6.7	1.6										34
11. Job satisfaction	6.3	1.8										

[a]All coefficients are significant at *p* < .01 or better. As noted in Chapter 2, the potential range of mean scores is from 1 to 9.

TABLE 3.10
Subordinates' Means, Standard Deviations (SD), and Correlations for the Social Service Sample ($N = 117$)[a]

Scale	Mean	SD	2	3	4	5	6	7	8	9	10	11
Communication style												
1 Careful transmitter	6.3	1.2	47	34	38	25	38	49	43	32	50	20*
2 Open and two-way	6.1	1.6		43	42	39	59	55	41	55	66	32
3 Frank	6.3	1.4			21*	51	30	44	53	39	43	18
4 Careful listener	7.7	1.0				38	50	57	15**	42	59	28
5 Informal	6.5	1.7					57	31	38	20	37	08**
Credibility												
6 Trustworthy	7.4	1.5						53	39	34	67	29
7 Informative	7.6	1.5							56	46	78	36
8 Dynamic	6.9	1.2								41	53	22*
Outcomes												
9 Role clarity	7.2	1.2									61	47
10 Satisfaction with focal person	6.8	1.4										39
11 Job satisfaction	5.6	1.9										

[a]Coefficients with two asterisks are not significant; those with one asterisk are significant at $p < .05$. The remaining are significant at $p < .01$ or better. As noted in Chapter 2, the potential range of mean scores is from 1 to 9.

model have broad applicability and can be used to indentify specific interpersonal communication dimensions and their impacts in various organizational settings.

In the next chapter, we will report results pertaining to the extent to which the model is able to predict impacts of consequence.

4

Application of the Model
in Three Organizations

The preceding chapters presented the underlying conceptual rationale for the communication model and methodological and statistical issues concerning our measures. We turn now to some empirical data from the three organizations described in the previous chapter—the information technology firm; the Navy civilian agency; and the social service agency. We will be examining these data from several perspectives. In so doing, we will further elaborate on specific methodological and statistical issues that pertain to the analyses.

Three related types of analyses will be employed to test the model: partial correlation analysis, regression analysis, and path analysis. As indicated in Chapter 3, these approaches cannot prove the causal linkages proposed in the two-stage communication model. However, they can tell us something about the model's ability to predict certain outcomes. Each analysis will be replicated in the three organizations.

Our concern in this chapter is with the focal person and how that individual is *generally* perceived by subordinates in the work setting. Thus in the analyses reported here, we utilized data only from subordinate colleagues of a given focal person and excluded other colleague data (peers, superiors). A mean score of subordinates' responses for a given focal person was first calculated, and this value in turn became a data point for a particular analysis. As suggested in

Chapter 3 (and shown by the analysis reported in Table 3.7), colleague responses did discriminate between focal persons, as opposed to merely projecting the respondents' own needs, preferences, biases, or generalized views of interpersonal communication, credibility, and outcomes. Hence, the use of mean scores seems appropriate, particularly since we are most concerned at this point with the focal person rather than with the individual variation that may exist between colleagues of a focal person. This latter issue will be addressed in subsequent chapters.

Underlying Hypotheses and Results

As a way of clarifying the proposed causal linkages in the communication model, we will examine each link in a sequential manner in terms of the following hypothesis testing framework.

Hypothesis 1

Hypothesis: A focal person's communication style will be a significant predictor of perceived credibility (as measured by trustworthiness, informativeness, and dynamism) of the focal person.

As sketched at the top of the model in Figure 3.1, in testing this hypothesis, the communication style variables were used as the independent variable predictors of each of the three credibility factors. Three separate multiple regression runs were performed for each of the credibility measures for each organization. A regression routine (SPSS) that employs the standard regression method (each variable is treated as if it is being added to the regression equation after all other variables are included) was utilized in this analysis. (Subsequently for Hypothesis 4, stepwise regression was used to examine the independent contribution of credibility in predicting the outcomes in the model.)

Results. The results are presented in Tables 4.1–4.3. As can be seen, the hypothesis is generally supported for each credibility measure in the three samples. All the F values were significant at the .01 level

TABLE 4.1
Multiple Regressions (Communication Style Predicting Trustworthy) for
Three Organizations

	Dependent variable (*trustworthy*)		
Independent variables (communication style)	Information technology firm ($N = 325$)	Navy civilian agency ($N = 57$)	Social service agency ($N = 25$)
Careful listener	.04	.09	.78**
Informal	.55**	.45**	.54**
Careful transmitter	.00	.07	−.05
Open and two-way	.35**	.04	.28*
Frank	−.22**	.02	−.19
F	91.4**	10.3**	26.7**
Multiple R	.73	.71	.94
R^2 (adjusted)[a]	.53(.53)	.50(.45)	.88(.84)

[a]The number in parentheses is the adjusted R^2 statistic that adjusts for the number of independent variables and number of cases involved in the analysis, and hence is a more conservative estimate of the amount of variance explained. The formula used here is:

$$\text{Adjusted } R^2 = R^2 - [(k - 1)/(N - k)](1 - R^2)$$

where k is the number of independent variables, N is the sample size, and R^2 is the unadjusted R^2 (Nie, Hull, Jenkins, Steinbrenner, & Bent, 1975, p. 358). Subsequent tables (4.2–4.11) also report the adjusted R^2 value using the same formula.
*$p < .05$.
**$p < .01$.

(except dynamic in the social service sample), with 16–84% of the variance accounted for across organizations. The optimum composite of communication style variables and the three measures of credibility were with trustworthy and informative (where the adjusted R^2's ranged from .31 to .84), while the amount of variance explained for dynamic as a dependent variable was somewhat less (16–40%).

Frank was the most consistent predictor across samples and credibility variables, followed by informal, open and two-way, and careful listener. Interestingly, frank was a positive predictor of informative and dynamic, whereas for trustworthy it had a significant negative effect in one of the organizations. While this pattern is understandable, it poses an interesting problem in that frank communication appears to have a conflicting effect. It suggests that some trade-offs are involved in being frank. The same may be the case for careful listener, which negatively

TABLE 4.2
Multiple Regressions (Communication Style Predicting Informative) for Three Organizations

Independent variables (communication style)	Dependent variable (*informative*)		
	Information technology firm ($N = 325$)	Navy civilian agency ($N = 57$)	Social service agency ($N = 25$)
Careful listener	.06	−.06	.92**
Informal	.14*	.07	−.03
Careful transmitter	.20**	.28	.05
Open and two-way	.26**	.22	.16
Frank	.24**	.32*	−.15
F	53.5**	6.1**	5.8**
Multiple R	.68	.61	.77
R^2 (adjusted)	.46(.45)	.37(.31)	.60(.50)

*$p < .05$.
**$p < .01$.

TABLE 4.3
Multiple Regressions (Communication Style Predicting Dynamic) for Three Organizations

Independent variables (communication style)	Dependent variable (*dynamic*)		
	Information technology firm ($N = 325$)	Navy civilian agency ($N = 57$)	Social service agency ($N = 25$)
Careful listener	−.32**	−.08	−.16
Informal	−.07	.00	.30
Careful transmitter	.07	.06	.14
Open and two-way	.24**	.00	.03
Frank	.54**	.39**	.07
F	43.5**	4.7**	1.9
Multiple R	.64	.46	.58
R^2 (adjusted)	.41(.40)	.21(.16)	.34(.16)

**$p < .01$.

predicted dynamic as might be expected but had a positive impact on informative and trustworthy.

Hypothesis 2

Hypothesis: A focal person's credibility as communicator will be a significant predictor of the following outcomes: satisfaction with focal person, job satisfaction, role clarity, and effectiveness.

This hypothesis thus examines the second linkage from the intervening variables (focal person credibility) to the consequences of concern (our dependent variables). In testing this linkage, the three credibility measures (trustworthy, informative, and dynamic) served as independent variables. Separate regressions were run on each of the dependent measures for each sample. For this analysis, an effectiveness scale for the work unit supervised by the focal person was available only for the information technology firm.

Results. The results of the analysis are reported in Step 1 of Tables 4.4–4.7. Eight of the 10 F values were significant at $p < .05$ or better, thus providing support for the stated hypothesis. Trustworthy and informative were quite consistently significant. An examination of the R^2 values indicates that by far the strongest impact of the credibility measures was on satisfaction with focal person (adjusted R^2 s ranged from .68 to .87), with considerably less variance accounted for in the other dependent variable measures.

In addition to testing the above sets of linkages proposed by our model, the relationship between focal person's communication style and the consequences was also examined more directly as a hypothesis in the following terms.

Hypothesis 3

Hypothesis: A focal person's communication style will be a significant predictor of the following outcomes: satisfaction with focal person, job satisfaction, subordinate colleague role clarity, and effectiveness.

TABLE 4.4
Stepwise Multiple Regressions for Three Organizations with Role Clarity as
Dependent Variable

Independent variable	Information technology firm ($N= 325$)	Navy civilian agency ($N = 57$)	Social service agency ($N = 25$)
Step 1			
Trustworthy	−.31**	.22*	.09
Informative	.36**	.14	.07
Dynamic	.07	.09	.06
F	58.2**	5.4*	1.7
Multiple R	.59	.48	.44
R^2 (adjusted)	.35(.35)	.23(.19)	.20(.08)
Step 2			
Trustworthy	.16*	.16	.05
Informative	.22**	.08	−.19
Dynamic	.02	.10	.32*
Careful listener	.02	.02	.25
Informal	.02	−.05	−.22
Careful transmitter	.02	.23	.00
Open and two-way	.30**	−.06	.28**
Frank	.04	.04	−.03
F	28.0**	2.7	4.4
Multiple R	.64	.56	.80
R^2 (adjusted)	.41(.40)	.31(.20)	.64(.50)
R^2 change	.06**	.08	.44**

*$p < .05$.
**$p < .01$.

The same multiple regression analysis was perfomed with the five communication style variables as predictors in separate regression runs for each of the outcome variables.

Results. As can be seen in Tables 4.8–4.11, the hypothesis was supported for all four outcome measures across the three organizations. Once again, satisfaction with focal person had the greatest amount of explained variance, with adjusted R^2 values ranging from .63 to .73. Next came role clarity, followed by job satisfaction and effectiveness. The most consistent communication style predictor variable was open and two-way, with informal, careful transmitter, and careful listener showing occasional strength.

TABLE 4.5
Stepwise Multiple Regressions for Three Organizations with Job Satisfaction as Dependent Variable

Independent variables	Information technology firm ($N = 325$)	Navy civilian agency ($N = 57$)	Social service agency ($N = 25$)
Step 1			
Trustworthy	.26**	.28	.20
Informative	.34**	.12	.30
Dynamic	.06	−.08	.00
F	42.0**	2.1	5.4*
Multiple R	.53	.32	.58
R^2 (adjusted)	.28(.28)	.10(.05)	.33(.27)
Step 2			
Trustworthy	.19**	.19	.65*
Informative	.30**	.02	.07
Dynamic	.06	−.17	.28
Careful listener	.09	−.24	−.26
Informal	−.09	.20	−.37
Careful transmitter	−.14*	−.03	−.36
Open and two-way	.25**	.23	.27
Frank	−.03	.18	−.25
F	19.1*	1.7	2.9*
Multiple R	.57	.47	.77
R^2 (adjusted)	.33(.31)	.22(.09)	.59(.38)
R^2 change	.05**	.12	.26

*$p < .05$.
**$p < .01$.

Hypothesis 4

The remaining hypothesis looked more closely at the proposed causal sequence of linkages presented in the model and specifically tested the hypothesized importance of focal person credibility as a central, moderating factor that can explain how focal person communication behavior affects colleague behavior and attitudes. These relationships were expressed as follows.

Hypothesis: The independent contribution of focal person credibility will account for a significant amount of the

TABLE 4.6
Stepwise Multiple Regressions for Three Organizations with Satisfaction with
Focal Person as Dependent Variable

Independent variables	Information technology firm ($N = 325$)	Navy civilian agency ($N = 57$)	Social service agency ($N = 25$)
Step 1			
Trustworthy	.33**	.39**	.38**
Informative	.58**	.57**	.33**
Dynamic	.11**	−.05	.00
F	233.8**	44.3**	79.4**
Multiple R	.83	.85	.94
R^2(adjusted)	.69(.68)	.71(.70)	.88(.87)
Step 2			
Trustworthy	.13**	.11	.40*
Informative	.42**	.44**	.14
Dynamic	.08*	.02	.19
Careful listener	.10*	.16*	.29
Informal	.11**	.16*	−.16
Careful transmitter	.00	.15*	.00
Open and two-way	.27**	.09	.03
Frank	.03	−.04	.06
F	127.0**	32.4**	22.6**
Multiple R	.87	.92	.95
R^2 (adjusted)	.76(.76)	.84(.82)	.90(.86)
R^2 change	.07**	.13**	.02

*$p < .05$.
**$p < .01$.

**presumed relationship between the independent variables
and the following dependent variables: satisfaction with
focal person, job satisfaction, subordinate colleague role
clarity, and effectiveness.**

As an initial test of this hypothesis, the relationship between each
independent variable and the three dependent variable measures was
examined before and after the credibility variables were statistically
controlled (through partial correlation analysis). This was done separately for each of the three factors constituting focal person credibility
specified in the model as well as for all of them combined. If the model

TABLE 4.7

Stepwise Multiple Regression for Information Technology Firm with
Effectiveness as Dependent Variable

Independent variables	Information technology firm $(N = 325)$
Step 1	
Trustworthy	.34**
Informative	.18**
Dynamic	−.01
F	26.2**
Multiple R	.44
R^2 (adjusted)	.20(.19)
Step 2	
Trustworthy	.09
Informative	.28**
Dynamic	−.02
Careful listener	.07
Informal	.01
Careful transmitter	−.06
Open and two-way	.16*
Frank	.02
F	11.0**
Multiple R	.47
R^2 (adjusted)	.22(.20)
R^2 change	.02**

*$p < .05$.
**$p < .01$.

were correct, the partial correlations should be substantially lower in
magnitude than the direct or zero-order correlations between the
independent variables and the dependent variables.

Results. As can be seen in Table 4.12, the general pattern of zero-
order correlations compared with partial correlations (Column 1 versus
Column 2 for each organization) supported Hypothesis 4. That is, when
all three credibility variables were controlled, the correlations dropped
considerably and tended to be low and nonsignificant, except in a few
cases, such as for satisfaction with focal person in the information
technology firm and the Navy civilian agency, and for job satisfaction in
the social service agency.

A secondary analysis using stepwise multiple regression was also
performed as follows. First the block of three credibility variables was
introduced into the regression, followed by the addition of the block of

TABLE 4.8

Multiple Regressions (Communication Style Predicting Role Clarity) for Three Organizations

	Dependent variable (role clarity)		
Independent variables	Information technology firm ($N = 325$)	Navy civilian agency ($N = 57$)	Social service agency ($N = 25$)
Careful listener	.04	.02	.07
Informal	.14*	.03	−.08
Careful transmitter	.07	.27*	.03
Open and two-way	.42**	−.04	.27**
Frank	.07	.11	.00
F	37.4**	4.4**	6.0**
Multiple R	.61	.50	.74
R^2 (adjusted)	.37(.36)	.25(.18)	.54(.45)

*$p < .05$.
**$p < .01$.

TABLE 4.9

Multiple Regressions (Predicting Satisfaction with Focal Person) for Three Organizations

	Dependent variable (satisfaction with focal person)		
Independent variable (communication style)	Information technology firm ($N = 325$)	Navy civilian agency ($N = 57$)	Social service agency ($N = 25$)
Careful listener	.10*	.15	.71**
Informal	.23**	.24*	.11
Careful transmitter	.09*	.22*	.00
Open and two-way	.44**	.26*	.17
Frank	.14**	.11	−.03
F	111.6**	21.4**	16.8**
Multiple R	.80	.82	.88
R^2 (adjusted)	.65(.63)	.68(.65)	.77(.73)

*$p < .05$.
**$p < .01$.

TABLE 4.10
Multiple Regressions (Communication Style Predicting Job Statisfaction) for
Three Organizations

Independent variables (communication style)	Dependent variable (job satisfaction)		
	Information technology firm ($N = 325$)	Navy civilian agency ($N = 57$)	Social service agency ($N = 25$)
Careful listener	.10	−.21	.27
Informal	.05	.29	.06
Careful transmitter	−.08	−.02	−.36
Open and two-way	.41**	.24	.47*
Frank	.03	.12	−.36
F	20.4**	2.4*	2.7
Multiple R	.49	.44	.64
R^2 (adjusted)	.24(.23)	.19(.11)	.42(.26)

*$p < .05$.
**$p < .01$.

communication style variables as the second step in the regression.
If the credibility dimensions were to mediate the independent–
dependent variable relationship as predicted (a) the credibility
measures alone should account for a sizable portion of the explained
dependent variable variance; and (b) the introduction of the second
block of five communication style variables into the equation should
not substantially increase the amount of variance explained.[1]

The results of this analysis are presented in Tables 4.4–4.7, which
indicate that the introduction of the second set of predictors (Step 2
versus Step 1) did yield modest increases in the R^2 values in most
cases. Six of the 10 increases were statistically significant, though in
numerical terms they were mostly moderate in size.

Overall, these two analyses yielded mixed support for the hypothesis,

---

[1]The following formula was used to calculate whether the increases in the R^2s were
significant:

$$F = \frac{(R^2_{y.\,12\ldots k_1} - R^2_{y.\,12\ldots k_2})/(k_1 - k_2)}{(1 - R^2_{y.\,12\ldots k_1})/(N - k - 1)}$$

(Kerlinger and Pedhauzer, 1973, p. 71).

TABLE 4.11
Multiple Regression (Communication Style Predicting Effectiveness) for
Information Technology Firm

Independent variables (communication style)	Information technology firm ($N = 325$)
Careful listener	.09
Informal	.10
Careful transmitter	.00
Open and two-way	.26**
Frank	.05
F	17.1**
Multiple R	.42
R^2 (adjusted)	.17(.16)

*$p < .01$.

with the partial correlation analysis providing the most consistent
support for the prediction.

PATH ANALYSIS PERTINENT TO HYPOTHESIS 4

In addition to the preceding tests for Hypothesis 4, a path analysis
was also performed to further examine the relationships proposed in
the model. In particular, the concern was to explore the extent to which
simpler models might be obtained that supported the causal linkages
and that might yield close to the same amount of explained dependent
variable variance with fewer variables.

The path analysis involved the determination of the path coefficients
(standardized regression coefficients) for the hypothesized causal
paths. The general path diagram tested is as shown in Figure 4.1.

This set of relationships was proposed for each of the four dependent
variable measures, and hence the analysis involved an examination of
such a path diagram for each dependent variable and for each organizational setting.

The following procedure was employed for calculating the path
coefficients for each diagram:

1. Regress on C (consequence), on A (communication style vari-
    ables), and B (credibility variables). This provided path coeffi-
    cients from B to C.
2. Regress B on A. This provided the path coefficients from A
    to B.

TABLE 4.12

Partial Correlation Analysis (Relationship of Communication Style Variables to Consequence Variables) with and without Credibility Variables Held Constant[a,b]

Style variables	Information technology firm (N = 325)		Navy civilian agency (N = 54)		Social service agency (N = 23)	
	(1)	(2)	(1)	(2)	(1)	(2)
Satisfaction with Focal Person						
Careful transmitter	.44	.15	.66	.44	.57	.05*
Open and two-way	.74	.44	.61	.43	.56	.03*
Frank	.53	.21	.48	.15*	−.07*	.02*
Careful listener	.51	.31	.66	.56	.83	.33*
Informal	.61	.25	.70	.49	.48	−.24*
Job Satisfaction						
Careful transmitter	.18	.07*	17	−.02*	.20*	−.20*
Open and two-way	.48	.19	.32	.21*	.54	.34*
Frank	.26	.00*	.31	.25	−.30*	−.33*
Careful listener	.31	.09*	.12	−.08*	.36	−.31*
Informal	.33	.02*	.33	.16*	.10*	−.44
Role Clarity						
Careful transmitter	.33	.08*	.49	.31	.43	.23*
Open and two-way	.58	.31	.21*	−.02*	.71	.54
Frank	.38	.15	.28	.05*	−.18*	−.24*
Careful listener	.37	.13	.34	.14*	.35	.04*
Informal	.44	.09*	.36	.08*	.09*	−.01*
Effectiveness						
Careful transmitter	.20	.02*				
Open and two-way	.39	.07*				
Frank	.25	.07*				
Careful listener	.31	.05*				
Informal	.32	.02*				

[a](1) = zero-order correlation; (2) = holding all credibility variables constant.

[b]All coefficients are significant except those with an asterisk.

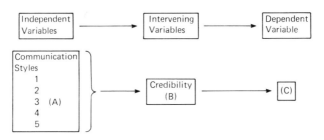

Figure 4.1. General path diagram.

After performing the initial analysis as outlined here for a given diagram, the resulting path coefficients were examined to see if a simplified model could be obtained. Paths with coefficients less than or equal to .15 were dropped, as well as any paths where the coefficients might be greater than .15 but nonsignificant. The resulting models for each dependent variable in each organization are presented in Figures 4.2–4.4. In discussing the results from this analysis, each of the dependent variable measures is considered sequentially for the pattern of results across the three organizations.

Role Clarity. Figures 4.2–4.4 reveal the results for role clarity as the consequence. Overall the explained variance (R^2) was relatively similar across organizations, ranging from .19 to .35. In all cases, dynamic dropped out of the analysis, leaving trustworthy and informative as the significant intervening variables in the model. The five communication measures were retained as predictors of credibility in only one case

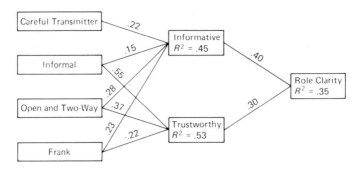

Figure 4.2. Path analysis for information technology firm on role clarity ($N = 325$).

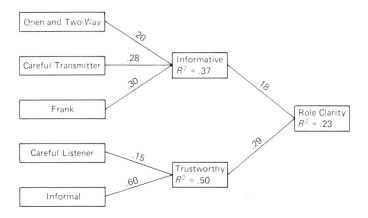

Figure 4.3. Path analysis for Navy civilian agency on role clarity ($N = 57$).

(the Navy civilian agency), while for the information technology firm, careful listener dropped out, and in the social service sample, careful transmitter and frank were eliminated. Open and two-way and informal were quite consistently the stronger predictors. Not surprisingly, careful listener was a particularly strong predictor for the social service organization, where such a skill is inherent in the organization's mission.

Job Satisfaction. The explained variance for this outcome was less strong than for role clarity, with R^2's ranging from .10 to .33 (see Figures 4.5–4.7). Once again dynamic dropped out, and informative was also eliminated in one case (the Navy civilian agency). Trustworthy was the most consistent predictor. Among the five communication variables, informal was represented in all diagrams, while careful

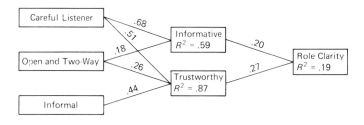

Figure 4.4. Path analysis for social service agency on role clarity ($N = 25$).

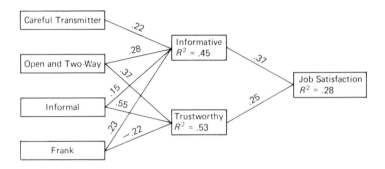

Figure 4.5. Path analysis for information technology firm on job satisfaction ($N = 325$).

listener was included in two of the three diagrams. In general, the explained variance obtained with the path analysis was reasonably close to that obtained when all variables were included in the prediction equation see (Table 4.5).

Satisfaction with Focal Person. The amount of variance explained for this outcome was quite strong, ranging from .68 to .88 (see Figures 4.8–4.10). Informative and trustworthy were consistently the best credibility predictors. Dynamic dropped out completely for all three organizations. Among the five communication style variables, careful listener dropped out in one instance (the information technology firm), as did careful transmitter and frank (social service sample). Informal was the strongest predictor of trustworthy, and open and two-way was the most consistent predictor of informative. The R^2 values for satisfaction were quite close to those obtained when all variables were entered (see Table 4.6).

Effectiveness. Data on this outcome were collected only for the information technology firm. As indicated in Figure 4.11, dynamic

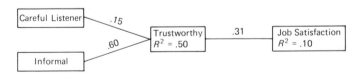

Figure 4.6. Path analysis for Navy civilian agency on job satisfaction ($N = 57$).

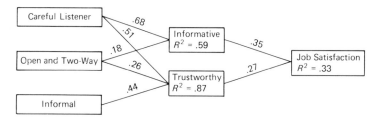

Figure 4.7. Path analysis for social service agency on job satisfaction ($N = 25$).

dropped out in the analysis as did careful listener. The obtained R^2 was very close to that derived when all variables were included in the prediction equation (see Table 4.7).

Discussion and Summary

As seen in Figures 2–4, in all three organizations, the extent to which subordinate colleagues felt a clear sense of role clarity correlated with how much the focal person was seen to be informative and trustworthy. Whether they were dynamic or not was irrelevant. What it took for a focal person to be informative depended on the organization. Careful listening helped in the social service setting. Open and two-way communication was important to being seen as informative in all three

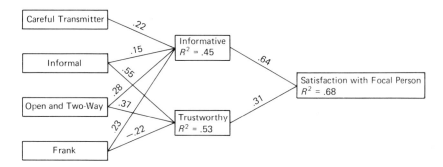

Figure 4.8. Path analysis for information technology firm on satisfaction with focal person ($N = 325$).

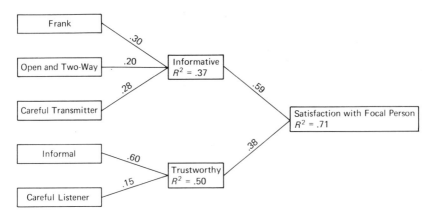

Figure 4.9. Path analysis for Navy civilian agency on satisfaction with focal person ($N =$ 57).

organizations. Frankness also contributed to being seen as informative in two organizations.

The pattern of communication variables that contributed to trustworthiness likewise depended on the organization in which the focal person and subordinate colleagues were located. In the information technology firm, informality and openness were particularly important. In the Navy civilian agency, only careful listening and informality were important to trustworthiness. Again in the social service sample, informality contributed to trustworthiness, but this time in combination with open and two-way communication.

Although job satisfaction was a consequence of informativeness and trustworthiness in the information technology firm and social service

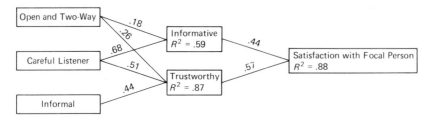

Figure 4.10. Path analysis for social service agency on satisfaction with focal person ($N = 25$).

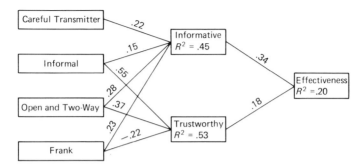

Figure 4.11. Path analysis for information technology firm on effectiveness ($N = 325$).

sample, in the Navy civilian agency, it was most important to be trustworthy. And of course, the communication behaviors contributing to credibility factors of informativeness and trustworthiness remained as before.

It should be noted that the fact that satisfaction with focal person had the largest explained variance associated with it (compared to the other outcome variables) may be accounted for in part at least by a potential leniency influence that may be operating. Thus, colleagues (especially subordinates) who may like their focal person for reasons not directly due to that person's communication style and credibility may therefore also be inclined to rate the focal person more favorably on the communication and credibility dimensions as well. The extent to which this leniency effect exists cannot be readily discerned or partialled out in a straightforward manner and is a problem that much of the research employing survey instruments of the sort used here must contend with. As indicated in a later analysis in Chapter 10, it is evident that at least some of the explained variance with regard to satisfaction with focal person may in fact be attributed to this source. Additional perspectives and approaches in dealing with the issue are also discussed in that chapter.

In conclusion, the pattern of results in the analyses reported in this chapter provides general support for the model proposed in Chapter 2. Of the three measures of credibility, it seems clear that being seen as informative and trustworthy are the most important credibility dimensions, while being dynamic is not important. All five communication variables emerge as relevant in different circumstances across organizations, credibility dimensions, and outcome measures, thus reinforcing the general applicability of the five factors of communication style in organizational settings. Yet to be examined, however, are some additional contextual factors (e.g., technology and size) that may influence the relationships involved here. These issues are dealt with in the next several chapters.

5

Context and Content Factors
Influencing Communication

In the immediately preceding chapters, we have addressed ourselves to communication as if it were merely a matter between senders and receivers. Yet as noted in Chapter 1, previous research has strongly suggested that the content and the context of messages are important for understanding the communication process. In the present chapter, we will look at how situation, medium, and message affect communication style, credibility, and their impact.

We expected that if a focal person and colleague can, and do, communicate by intercom or face to face whenever they want, the communications of the focal person as seen by the colleague are likely to be systematically different than if they must meet and if these meetings are infrequent. Focal persons who spend time talking about personal matters would be seen differently by colleagues than focal persons who never discuss personal or social matters but only job-related issues with colleagues. Systematic differences were also expected if colleagues and focal persons are at the same rather than at different organizational levels.

In Chapters 3 and 4, we have seen that, as a whole, ignoring the context or content of the communication, subordinate colleagues are satisfied with a focal person judged by them to be trustworthy and informative. For a focal person judged by subordinate colleagues as trustworthy in turn depends on the focal person's being seen as open and two-way, a careful listener, and informal in style. To be judged informative depends on being seen as open and two-way and frank. Style and credibility contribute to role clarity and satisfaction with focal person.

In this chapter, we expand our focus beyond subordinate colleagues and include the peers and superiors of a focal person as well. We will examine the extent to which content and context can make a difference in these relationships and how communication style, credibility, and impact of a focal person on colleagues (peers and superiors as well as subordinates) are affected by factors influencing the potential for interaction, such as the distance between focal person and colleague physically, organizationally, personally, socially, and sociologically (see Figure 5.1). Singled out for attention by Bass (1960) in predicting the likelihood that two individuals would interact were group size, geographical proximity, social proximity, contact opportunity, intimacy and familiarity, mutuality of esteem and attraction, and homogeneity in abilities and attitudes.

We are also concerned with whether the linkages in effects between context and communication are direct or indirect. For example, the physical distance between focal persons and their colleagues may directly impact on the style of communication. Thus, Form (1972) noted that interactions among employees were related to the density of colleagues in the work area and their interpersonal proximity. Similarily, physical distance may affect the tendency to use one medium of communication rather than another, say the telephone rather than face-to-face communication. This greater use of the telephone in turn may increase the extent the focal person is judged to be a

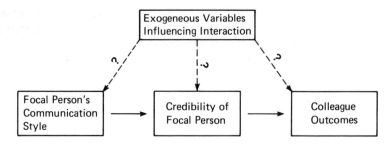

Figure 5.1. Possible impact of variables influencing interaction on original communication model.

careful listener and hence trustworthy. Again, organizational rather than physical distance may result in more written than verbal interchanges, reducing the likelihood of being judged as frank and hence informative. Conrath (1973a) had tested the extent to which telephone usage increased with distance. Surprisingly, he had failed to find supporting evidence, probably because he had not controlled for organizational differences. However, he did discover distance contributed to more written communications and fewer face-to-face communications as would be expected intuitively.

Research Related to Context and Content

Effects of Distance

Gullahorn (192) reported that distance was most important in determining the frequency of interaction among employees. Bass (1960) reviewed what was known up to 1959 about the general tendencies of people to interact as a function of physical, psychological, and social distance among individuals. The tendency to interact, "interaction potential," was seen by Bass to affect the effectiveness of working relations between individuals. Monge and Kirste (1975) extended the examination of proximity as a time-and-space opportunity, again showing its positive association with the potential to interact and satisfaction with the interaction.

Using ecco analysis, in which respondents report whether or not they have received a particular message and the immediate source of the message, Davis (1968) showed that organizational distance makes a difference in the extent informal communications for a particular oral message will be received. Thus, the percentage of assistant foremen and foremen at lower levels who reported receiving information about parking or layoffs originated by the top of the organization was less than reported by higher level supervision.

Effects of Size

Bass (1960) found generally among many investigations that the size of one's network directly affected the potential to interact with any one member of the network. Thus, Donald (1959) noted that the increased physical size of an organization decreased communications from its officers to its members. Again, O'Reilly and Roberts (1977) reported in three similar U.S. Naval organizations containing 407 personnel a correlation of −.67 between work group size and the extent its members communicated with each other. As Bass (1960) had noted, they inferred that "as group size increased, the possibility for group connectedness decreased because of limitations on the amount of effort that an individual can spend interacting with an increasing number of others [p. 677]." The quality of the communications was also affected by contextual circumstances. Open communication between members was greater for groups whose members were higher in organizational level and who were more likely to interact with each other. Such open communication contributed to group effectiveness.

While these distance and size variables describing the context of an interaction are conceptually related, they are nevertheless empirically distinct. For purposes of examination, we have organized them into two sets: context variables relating to notions of distance (physical, organizational, personal, and social) and context variables relating to the potential for contact (contact possibilities) as influenced by the number of people in a focal person's work surroundings.

Effects of Content

Content can also make a difference. The drop-off at lower levels from higher levels in receipt of messages in Davis's (1968) ecco analyses was more severe for routine information about parking than for information about layoffs relevant to production. Elsewhere, Davis (1953) showed that, the higher the interest value of an oral communication, the more likely it is to be passed up and down the line. With a different method, Wickesberg (1968) found similar filtering due to organizational distance in a study of all communications among 91 businessmen during a 5-day period.

Walton (1963) suggested that different focal persons are likely to attract to themselves messages of different kinds of content although little evidence is available to support the proposal (Monge *et al.*, 1978).

We will also look at the extent to which these context variables are affected by the medium of communication used, the content of such interchange, and in turn, the impact of the medium and content on a focal person's communication style, credibility, and its consequences.

Assessing Distance, Contact, Medium, and Content

A total of 577 civilian employees of a Navy civilian agency (the same one as in Chapter 4) located in a large urban area completed colleague questionnaires for selected focal persons. The rate of return of the questionnaires was over 80%. A variety of physical and non-physical measures of distance between focal person and colleagues were extracted. Other measures dealt with how often the communications between focal person and colleagues employed different media and were about different kinds of content.

These variables would be expected to vary considerably for different colleagues of the same focal person. Hence for the present analyses, we have treated each colleague (whether he or she was a subordinate, peer, or superior of the focal person) as a unit of analysis rather than utilizing a mean score for a given focal person as was done in Chapter 4.

Measures of Distance

Guided by the preceding discussion of variables likley to affect the potential to interact, we formulated a variety of measures of physical, social, and personal distance. We hypothesized that the greater the distance between the colleagues and the focal persons they described, the less the propensity to interact. In turn, this reduced potential to interact should systematically affect the style, credibility, and effectiveness of the interaction.

ORGANIZATIONAL DISTANCE

This measure was operationalized as the number of levels in the organizational separating the focal person's position from that of the responding colleague. In 35% of the cases, colleagues were at the same level as the focal person they described. In 49% of the cases, the focal person was the immediate superior or immediate subordinate of the colleague. In 16% of the cases, the focal person was more than one level higher up or lower down than the colleague. Of the 577 cases, 16 were described as "out of the organization" and were omitted from this analysis of organizational distance.

We hypothesized that subordinate–peer and peer–superior correlations in rating the same focal persons would be higher than subordinate–superior relationships. Subordinates and peers, and peers and superiors, were only one organizational level apart; subordinates and superiors were two levels apart.

Mean level differences in assigning ratings to focal persons were also expected. We hypothesized that in general focal persons deal with their subordinates differently than they communicate with their peers and superiors.

PHYSICAL DISTANCE

The collegial respondent's estimate of distance between his or her desk or work space and that of the focal person provided the measure of physical distance. Sixty-six percent of colleagues were close, within 100 feet of the focal person; 17% were over 100 feet, but on the same floor; 11% were on different floors, but in the same building; and 6% were in different buildings.

PERSONAL DISTANCE

Personal distance was measured by the responses to three questions. The first question asked about familiarity: "How well do you know the focal person?" Responses were as follows: (a) a little (5%); (b) some (28%); (c) considerably (48%); (d) very much (19%); and (e) completely (1%).[1]

The second question asked about length of acquaintanceship: "How long have you been associated with the focal person?" Responses were as follows: (a) under 6 months (9%); (b) 6 months to a year (11%); (c) 1–2 years (25%); and (d) over 2 years (56%).

The third question asked: "How often do you interact with the focal person during a typical week?" Responses were as follows: (a) once in a while (10%); (b) sometimes (17%); (c) fairly many times (24%); (d) very frequently (32%); and (e) continually (18%). (The alternatives were based on Bass et al.'s 1974 magnitude estimation scales of intensity and extensivity.)

Personal distance between focal person and colleagues was deemed

[1]Percentages may not add to 100 because of roundings.

greater with less familiarity, acquaintanceship, and frequency of contact.

SOCIAL DISTANCE

Communication patterns were also thought to be affected by the social distance between focal person and colleague (i.e., the difference in age, sex, and years of education). Analysis of age differences indicated that 32% of colleagues were the same age as the focal person they described, 30% were a year apart, and 19% were 4–7 years apart. Only 19% were more than 7 years apart in age. This small range of differences in age reduced the likelihood that much effect would be observed.

In looking at sex differences, 79% of colleagues were the same sex as the focal persons described, while 21% were of opposite sex.

As with age differences, educational differences between most colleagues and focal persons were not large. The median difference was 1.2 years. Only 10% were 4–9 years apart.

Measures of Contact Possibilities

Four measures of the size of collectivities in which the focal persons were located in time and space were obtained: (a) the size of their department; (b) the size of their work group; (c) the number of persons reporting to them; and (d) mobility—the number of promotions, transfers, and demotions of the focal person during the past 4 years. We deemed these four measures as indicative of the contact possibilities of the individual focal person.

Bass (1960) had attempted to account for the impact of group size on interaction potential and its consequences. At a given point in time, the more contact possibilities a focal person had, the less likely he or she would be to contact a designated colleague. (If I have connections with 15 people, I can contact *a specific one of them* more easily and frequently than if I have connections with 150 people.)

Mobility of a focal person was expected to have an impact on the focal person's style and credibility for other reasons as well. Thus, highly mobile aspirants have been found to send less accurate information upward even when high trust prevails (Athanassiades, 1973; Read, 1962). Here we were examining those who were actually more upwardly mobile. Presumably, their frankness and credibility should be affected if such mobility meant they were more inclined to tell their bosses what their bosses wanted to hear rather than what they needed to hear.

The median department size of focal persons was 30.0. The median work group size was 8.2. The frequencies for the number of persons directly reporting to a focal person were distributed as follows: 0, 33%; 1–5, 47%; 6–10, 12%; 11–15, 4%; 16–20, 1%; more than 20, 3%.

As for mobility, 33% of the 577 respondents had not changed positions at all in 4 years; 36% had experienced one change; 17%, two changes; 12%, three changes; and 1%, four changes in position.

Medium

Which medium was used to communicate was obtained by asking colleagues to indicate what percentages of the total 100% of communications they received from their focal person were in a particular mode. Average usage was as follows: written, 14%; face to face alone, 55%; in a group, 22%; and telephone, 6%.

Content

The content of the communications was obtained by asking colleagues to indicate the percentages of the total 100% of communications received from their focal person that dealt with each of three types of information: job, organizational, personal–social.

As has been noted many times before (Luthans, 1973), most managers spend most of their time receiving or transmitting job and organizational information. Only a small portion is non-task or non-organizational related. Consistent with earlier investigations, mean distribution of the content here was as follows: immediate job–task related, 65%; other organizational related, 14%; and personal or social, 19%.

Communication Model

Results for the communication model variables were derived from colleagues' ratings of the questionnaire items for behavior about a focal person in the same way as in preceding chapters. Table 5.1 lists the

TABLE 5.1
Colleagues' Ratings of Focal Persons' Communication Style, Credibility, and Consequences for Navy Civilian Agency $(N = 577)^a$

Rating of focal person by colleagues	Mean[b]	SD	Coefficient alpha
Communication style			
Careful transmitter	6.3	1.4	.82
Open, two-way	6.1	1.4	.77
Frank	6.5	1.4	.71
Careful listener	7.4	1.3	.87
Informal	6.8	1.7	.74
Credibility			
Trustworthy	7.6	1.4	.89
Informative	7.5	1.6	.94
Dynamic	7.0	1.4	.85
Outcomes			
Role clarity	7.4	1.2	.83
Job satisfaction	6.2	1.8	.80
Satisfaction with focal person	6.7	1.5	.91

[a]Because of missing values, the number of cases for each scale varied from 509 to 577.

[b]As in all data presentations, the potential range of scores is from 1 to 9, after transformation as described in Chapter 2.

variables, their means, and standard deviations for the 577 Navy civilian colleagues included in the analysis.

Interrelations among Measures of Distance, Contact, Medium, and Content

Table 5.2 shows the intercorrelations among the 19 context and content variables. Only those significant at the .01 level of confidence $(r = .11)$ are displayed. The meaning of these correlations will be discussed in the framework of factor scores.

Factor Analysis

In perfoming the factor analysis, one of the four media (percentage group) was omitted in order to eliminate artifactual negative relations

TABLE 5.2

Intercorrelations among Measures of Distance between Focal Persons and Colleagues, Contact Possibilities, Medium of Communications Used, and Content ($N = 577$ Colleagues)[a]

	Distance	Personal proximity				Social distance		
	(1) Org	(2) Phs	(3) Fam	(4) Acq	(5) Frq	(6) Age	(7) Sex	(8) Edu
Distance								
(1) Organizational							.11	
(2) Physical					−.14			
Personal proximity								
(3) Familiarity				.39	.37			
(4) Acquaintance-ship								
(5) Frequency interaction								
Social distance								
(6) Age difference							.18	.17
(7) Sex difference								.28
(8) Educational difference								
Contact possibilities								
(9) Department size								
(10) Work group size								
(11) No. persons reporting								
(12) Mobility								
Medium								
(13) Percentage written								
(14) Percentage face-to-face								
(15) Percentage group								
(16) Percentage telephone								
Content								
(17) Percentage job								
(18) Percentage Organizational								
(19) Percentage personal–social								

[a]With 575 df, $p < .01$ when $r = .11$. Only significant r's are shown.

Contact possibilities				Medium				Content		
(9) DpS	(10) WgS	(11) NPR	(12) Mob	(13) %Wr	(14) %FF	(15) %Gp	(16) %Ph	(17) %Job	(18) %Or	(19) %PS
	.15	.12		.24		−.22		.15		−.24
					−.23		.64			
			−.12					−.11		
								.11		
.12		.11								
		.12	.12							
			.24							
			.15	−.14	.11					
				−.39	−.22			.22		−.23
				−.54	−.54	−.30		.11	−.13	
								−.18	.19	.18
									−.46	−.72

that derive from a forced addition to 100% for the four variables. Similarly, since the three subjects of communication added to 100%, the two non-job-related variables (percentage organizational and percentage personal–social) were omitted from the factor analysis.

THE FACTORS

Seven interpretable factors emerged after varimax rotation for this sample. It should be clear that the factor structure is one that may be specific to this sample and organization. Different configurations may appear in other organizations. Only empirical study can tell. When all factors with eigenvalues above 1.0 were accepted, they accounted for 63.5% of the variance common to the 16 variables of the correlation matrix. Over 25 iterations were required in achieving solution of the varimax rotation. The factors and the percentages of the common variance (shown in parentheses) they accounted for were as follows:

I. *Percentage of Distant Communications* (12.3%)
   .86 % Telephone
   .74 % Physical Distance

This was a fairly obvious after-the-fact fallout. This dimension measures the extent colleagues communicate more often by telephone with their focal person and work further apart in physical distance.

II. *Percentage of Formal Communications* (10.9%)
   .86   % Written
   .17   Organizational Distance
   .57   % Face to Face Alone

This factor measures the tendency to write memos rather than meet face to face. It is slightly associated with organizational but not physical distance.

Rather than meet face to face, we telephone focal persons who are at our own organizational level but physically distant. However, instead of telephoning or meeting face to face, we send memos to persons at different organizational levels from us.

III. *Familiarity Due to Length of Acquaintanceship* (10.1%)
   .66 Length of Acquaintanceship
   .54 Familiarity

Familiarity is due to one of two separate and distinct reasons: length of acquaintanceship or frequency of contact. Factor III measures what is due to length of acquaintanceship. Factor VI measures how much is due to frequency of contact. Familiarity is common to the two factors.

IV. *Social Distance* (8.9%)
.52 Sex Difference
.47 Education Difference
.40 Age Difference
.19 Number of Persons Reporting
.18 Organizational Distance

Despite the small extent of sex, education, and age differences between focal persons and colleagues, the three differences clustered together in this sample. The resultant factor, IV, measured the combined effect of the three differences. One can readily imagine the typical high factor score generated by a younger, less educated female colleague lower in the organization describing an older, more educated male focal person. Colleague–focal person distance would also be likely to be higher. In addition, most probably, the older, better educated male would be at a higher organizational level.

V. *Larger Network* (7.7%)
.64 Mobility
.43 Work Group Size
.24 Number of Persons Reporting
.22 Organizational Distance

This factor measures the extent focal persons have an organizational space–time pattern containing a large number of persons. It measures whether they have moved around a lot in the organization during the past few years, currently are in a large organization, and have many persons reporting to them. As a member of such an enlarged network, the probabilities are increased for colleagues to be at different levels from the focal person. Organizational distances between focal person and colleague are greater in the aggregate.

VI. *Familiarity Due to Frequency of Interaction* (7.0%)
.68 Frequency of Interaction
.55 Familiarity

As was already mentioned when we looked at Factor III, we tend to interact with those we have known for longer periods of time. In addition, we tend to interact more with those with whom we are familiar; we avoid interaction with those with whom we are not familiar. Conversely, we become more familiar with those with whom we interact.

VII. *Percentage of Formal Content* (6.7%)

   .61   % Job Related

   .33   % Written

   .29   Organizational Distance

This factor measures the extent communications between focal persons and colleagues are formal—that is, about the job, not personal, social, or organizational; in writing, not face to face or in groups. Such formality is more likely where focal persons and colleagues are at different organizational levels.

In sum, given the results presented, we infer that obviously a colleague depends more on the telephone to communicate with a focal person the greater the physical distance between them. Such physical distance tends to reduce face-to-face communication and coincides with the organizational distance between colleagues and focal person.

In this sample, the same colleague–focal person pairs who differ in age are also likely to differ in sex and education and this again is more likely if the pair is at different organizational levels.

Colleagues reported themselves to be familiar with focal persons for one of two completely independent reasons: Either they had frequent contact with focal persons during the work week *or* they had been acquainted with the focal person for a long time. Familiarity due to frequent contact was slightly less likely if the focal person was physically distant from the colleagues. Familiarity due to such long-term acquaintanceship was less likely if the focal persons were highly mobile.

Highly mobile focal persons were also more likely to be in larger work groups, have more persons reporting to them, and be organizationally at greater distances from their colleagues, all conceptually placing them in larger communication networks.

Job-related communications were more likely to be written or face to face rather than by telephone and were more common between organizationally distant focal persons and colleagues. Presumably, organizationally close focal persons and colleagues communicated proportionately more frequently about social or personal content.

Scale scores for each colleague were calculated on each factor by weighting specific measures included in a factor scale by their factor loadings for that scale. For example, Factor I, percentage of distant communications, was calculated by summing the optimally weighted scores for physical distance and use of the telephone.

Content, Context, and Communication Styles

Communication style was largely independent of content or context. Organizational distance ($r = .11$) and physical distance ($r = .10$) appeared to contribute slightly[2] to being observed by colleagues as a careful transmitter. At the same time, careful listening was seen by colleagues slightly less frequently in focal person when work groups were larger ($r = -.11$) and more persons reported to the focal person ($r = -.11$). Since these contextual conditions accounted for no more than 1% of the variance in any of the five communication style variables, it seemed fair to say that the highly reliable communication styles were independent of context and content and could only be attributed to consistent individual differences regardless of content or context.

Content, Context, and Credibility

Content and context accounted for a small percentage of the variance in credibility.

Trustworthiness

Trustworthiness of focal persons was seen as greater if they were judged by colleagues to be more familiar with them ($r = .11$). But

---

[2]With 575 degrees of freedom for the data in this section on content, context, and communication styles, a correlation of .10 was statistically significant at the .01 level of confidence.

acquaintance and frequent interaction by themselves made no significant difference. As might have been expected, judged trustworthiness of focal persons by their colleagues was significantly lower in larger work groups ($r = .14$). It was also significantly lower for more mobile focal persons ($r = -.15$) and in larger networks ($r = -.19$) but not in larger departments ($r = .11$). In this organization, one's department size appeared to operate differently in its effects on trustworthy communications than did other indicators of the size and complexity of one's communication network, such as one's immediate work group size or one's mobility.

Informativeness

The factor of familiarity due to length of acquaintanceship correlated .15 with informativeness. The factor of familiarity due to interaction frequency also contributed to perceptions of informativeness ($r = .13$). Familiarity with the focal person in general correlated .17 with being regarded as an informative focal person. But no other context or content measures were significantly related to being rated as informative.

Dynamic

A focal person was less likely to be seen as dynamic by colleagues in larger departments ($r = -.13$), but familiarity to colleagues slightly enhanced a focal person's ratings by colleagues for dynamism ($r = .10$). This was true whether familiarity was due to length of acquaintanceship ($r = .12$) or to frequent interaction ($r = .11$). Again, it is clear that individual differences are paramount and that context and content contribute little to a focal person's being seen by colleagues as dynamic.

Content, Context, and Outcomes

For peers and superiors of a focal person, some of the outcomes in the model (role clarity and job satisfaction) are not likely to be as directly shaped or influenced by the focal persons as for subordinates.

However, satisfaction with focal person would be relevant to all colleagues. Hence, we focus here only on this last outcome for peers, superiors, and subordinates.

Again, as with communication styles and credibility, only a small proportion of variance in outcomes was associated with content and context. Most of the variance could only be accounted for by individual differences. Rated familiarity maded a slight difference in satisfaction with focal persons. Colleagues were more satisfied with focal persons with whom they were more familiar ($r = .14$) because of either length of acquaintanceship ($r = .10$) or frequency of interaction ($r = .11$).

Analysis of Organizational Locus of Colleagues

Three samples were available in which analyses had been completed of ratings of 215 focal persons by their 1329 colleagues according to whether the raters were subordinates, peers, or superiors of the focal persons.

The samples reflected populations from organizations varying in the extent to which they were controlled by an authority–obedience hierarchy. At one extreme was a sample drawn from 69 military officers at two air bases, described by their 425 colleagues. (This sample is discussed further in Chapter 7.) At the other extreme were 29 social service agency professionals and their 158 colleagues. In between were 117 industrial managers and their 746 colleagues. (This last sample is treated in greater detail in Chapter 6.)

Interorganizational Comparisons

As seen in Table 5.3, which displays the mean ratings assigned to focal persons by their own subordinates, peers, and superiors, some general trends could be discerned across all organizations. Peers and superiors gave higher ratings than subordinates to focal persons as careful transmitters in all three organizations. Evidently, focal persons do not take as much time getting prepared to meet with subordinates as they do with peers or superiors. At the same time, informality and trust in focal persons were judged higher in all three organizations by peers and superiors.

But more often, the pattern emerging in mean ratings as a function of

TABLE 5.3

Means of Colleagues' Ratings of Focal Person according to Colleagues'
Organizational Relation to Focal Person[a]

	Social service (N = 29)					
Raters:	Subordinates (N = 111)		Peers (N = 24)		Superiors (N = 23)	
	Mean	SD	Mean	SD	Mean	SD
Communication style						
Careful transmitter	5.95	1.44	6.89	1.02	6.26	.91
Open and two-way	5.98	1.39	6.28	1.06	5.91	1.34
Frank	5.73	1.31	6.58	1.25	6.35	.77
Careful listener	7.18	1.23	7.44	1.23	7.67	.96
Informal	5.50	1.72	6.64	1.68	6.37	1.40
Credibility						
Trustworthy	6.95	1.29	7.58	1.31	7.30	1.48
Informative	7.44	1.27	7.72	1.09	7.53	1.30
Dynamic	6.88	1.14	7.25	1.31	6.79	.84
Outcomes						
Role clarity[b]	7.51	.88				
Satisfaction with focal person	6.83	.94	6.88	1.10	6.74	.98
Job satisfaction[b]	7.23	1.29				

[a]As in all data presentations, the potential range of scores is from 1 to 9, after
transformation as described in Chapter 2.

[b]Peer and superior ratings for role clarity and job satisfaction are not considered here
since they are expected to be much less influenced by the focal person than for subordinate
ratings.

the locus of the rater depended on the organization involved. In general
among the social serivce professionals, subordinates tended to give
lower ratings to their focal persons than did peers and superiors. In
comparison to subordinates or superiors as raters, peers gave focal
persons highest ratings for careful transmitter, open and two-way
communication, informality, trustworthiness, informativeness, and
dynamism. As might have been expected, superiors gave highest
ratings to focal persons for their careful listening.

Subordinates of military officers gave the officers highest ratings for
careful listening and dynamism, and were highest in role clarity
for subordinates in the three organizations. Relative to subordinate and
superiors, peers emphasized informality of focal persons. Superiors of

Industrial personnel ($N = 117$)						Military officers ($N = 69$)					
Subordinates ($N = 316$)		Peers ($N = 283$)		Superiors ($N = 147$)		Subordinates ($N = 305$)		Peers ($N = 74$)		Superiors ($N = 46$)	
Mean	SD	Mean	SD	Mean	SD	Mean	SD	Mean	SD	Mean	SD
5.90	1.16	6.24	1.12	6.45	1.21	6.11	1.22	6.31	1.19	6.43	1.30
6.05	1.26	6.16	1.14	6.27	1.13	6.13	1.11	6.06	.90	6.00	1.24
6.33	1.36	6.54	1.10	6.84	.94	6.53	1.19	6.55	1.07	6.57	1.11
7.51	1.02	7.35	1.11	7.39	1.05	7.61	1.00	7.44	.97	7.31	1.27
5.97	1.72	6.66	1.17	6.81	1.32	6.66	1.30	6.95	1.20	6.19	1.40
7.13	1.15	7.18	1.17	7.41	1.21	7.52	1.19	7.64	1.02	7.58	1.15
7.41	1.18	7.50	1.12	7.57	1.12	7.49	1.61	7.42	1.03	7.50	1.33
6.81	1.25	7.17	1.02	7.43	.91	7.15	1.34	6.88	1.13	7.09	1.01
7.17	.88					7.54	.94				
6.40	1.28	6.52	1.22	6.63	1.13	6.63	1.46	6.79	.96	6.74	1.21
6.70	1.30					6.43	1.56				

military officers gave highest ratings to focal persons as careful transmitters.

Organizational Distance

To what extent was agreement among raters of focal persons dependent on the organizational location of the colleagues with respect to the focal person? We hypothesized that agreement would be lowest if there were two levels of distance involved, that is, if we looked at agreement between subordinates and superiors of the focal persons. Agreement was expected to be higher between subordinates and peers, and between peers and superiors. Table 5.4 suggests that results were accounted for by other issues. They depended on which variables were evaluated.

For social service professionals, agreement was highest for dynamism and careful listening. For industrial managers, agreement was

TABLE 5.4
Correlations among Subordinates (S), Peers (P), and Bosses (B) of Focal Persons Rating the Same Focal Persons[a]

	Social service personnel (N = 29)			Industrial personnel (N = 117)			Military officers (N = 69)		
Levels apart:	1	1	2	1	1	2	1	1	2
	S–P	P–B	S–B	S–P	P–B	S–B	S–P	P–B	S–B
Communication style									
Careful transmitter	.46*	.09	−.05	.32**	.40**	.27**	.15	.39**	.29*
Open and two-way	.29	.07	−.08	.33**	.08	.28**	.02	.20	.31*
Frank	−.10	.24	.17	.35**	.21*	.40**	.24	.26	.16
Careful listener	.41	.53*	.28	.50**	.52**	.36**	.45**	.57**	.53**
Informal	.14	.21	.40	.38**	.31**	.28**	.23	.16	.16
Credibility									
Trustworthy	.26	.34	.33	.42*	.40**	.44**	.22	.51**	.47**
Informative	.25	.01	.10	.19	.27**	.27**	.43**	.38**	.47**
Dynamic	.48*	.48*	.34	.19	.41**	.41**	.41**	.41**	.51**
Outcomes									
Satisfaction with focal person	.36	.02	.46*	.27**	.34**	.43**	.35*	.45**	.56**

[a]Mean score values are used in the calculations. Thus, mean score values are first calculated for the peers of a focal person, which in turn are correlated with mean score values for subordinates, etc.

*p < .05.
**p < .01.

highest for dynamism and careful listening, For industrial managers, agreement was highest for trustworthiness of the focal person, informality, careful listening, frankness, careful transmitter, and satisfaction with focal person. For military officers, agreement was highest for careful listening, informativeness, and dynamism.

We infer, in general, from these findings that results will be decidedly different if obtained from subordinates, peers, and superiors.

Summary

The pattern of results reported in this chapter indicates that the exogenous factors pertaining to content and context do not appear to be particularly central to furthering our understanding of the operation of the variables included in our original communication model. But caution is required on this point as well. In other samples, greater impact might occur. For example, sex, age, and education were generally similar among our focal persons and colleagues here. Physical distances were small as a whole. In addition, considerable information was not captured in other areas pertaining to specific communication content. Thus, additional studies may be helpful in further assessing the potential for greater variation than was found here.

6

Effects of Organization

Current research in the field of organizational behavior reveals considerable confusion and uncertainty regarding the relationship between communication behavior and such variables as technology, structure, and organization size. Separately, each of these variables has been found to be of considerable importance in particular studies. However, potential linkages among these and related variables are yet to be clearly established. In the exploratory research reported in this chapter, some of these linkages involving technology, size, and communication behavior are considered.

Technology and Organizational Communication

The significance of technology as a central and defining characteristic of organizations has been quite amply documented (Aldrich, 1972; Comstock & Scott, 1977; Lawrence & Lorsch, 1967; Woodward, 1965), even though there is still some debate as to the relative importance of this variable in contrast to organization size (Hickson *et al.*, 1969; Mohr, 1971).

The Question of Level

One issue surrounding the technology question is the level at which organizational technology is (or should be) measured or classified. As noted in Chapter 1, previous research tends to place entire organizations into one category or another for purposes of analysis (e.g., Woodward, 1965), although other research suggests that such macro-level categorizations may make unrealistic assumptions of homogeneity between departmental units and subunits (horizontally and vertically) within the larger organization being categorized.

At least three organizational levels can be considered when applying the concept of technology: individual worker; subunit or departmental unit; larger organization (Comstock & Scott, 1977). Thus, for example, higher level units within a large R&D organization may be involved primarily in planning technological developments, while at the lower levels, technical aspects of testing specific applications may be the primary activity. Alternatively, we may find accountants working on rather routine financial matters in the finance unit within the R&D organization, while engineers and scientists make up the bulk of the organization. In such a situation, we might be particularly interested in learning the extent to which the accounting function is of consequence compared to the basic overriding technological thrust of the organization in influencing organizational communication and behavior across subunits regardless of the immediate task of the particular group.

Individual Positions

Up to now there has been relatively little research to help us understand these potential effects of technology on organizational communication. Yet we are aware that those working in different functions tend to receive different amounts of information and sometimes from different sources. Thus, Davis (1953) found that staff managers were generally more informed about company events than line managers, while Holland (1972) noted that scientists in R&D organizations depended considerably on communication and information from professional colleagues outside their own organizations. These findings suggest that the particular mode of operation, specific task, or way of doing one's job (R&D scientist, accountant, purchasing agent, etc.) is likely to increase certain kinds of communication behaviors and interactions and decrease others.

The kind of education and training one has received in preparation for specific kinds of jobs and professions are obviously likely to influence communication behavior and what information can be and will be processed (Dearborn & Simon, 1958; Mason & Mitroff, 1973; McKenney, 1971). Furthermore, even within functional and disciplinary areas, different personal characteristics (depending on status, motivation for upward mobility, etc.) may influence communication interaction. In short, macrolevel categorizations of organizations by technology type get at only a portion of the picture; intraorganizational factors also deserve attention.

Size of Organization and Communication

The relative importance of size as a key variable in gaining an understanding of organizations has been considered in a number of studies. While much of the research has looked at the relationship of size to structure, other research has documented the importance of size as a variable for consideration in relation to communication behavior. Thomas and Fink's 1963 review of empirical research indicated that group size can significantly affect aspects of individual and group performance, member satisfaction, the nature of interaction, and the distribution of participation of group members. Subsequent field research provides support for these conclusions (e.g., Blau, 1968; Roberts & O'Reilly, 1974a). While the level of analysis of primary concern in examining the relationship of size to individual communication behavior has usually been the work group, other size considerations (number and size of departments as well as total organization size) might also influence the intensity and direction of flow. So despite our minimal results with work group size reported in the preceding chapter we again looked at size in two additional organizations and in different structural units.

In this chapter, we will examine the extent to which some of these technology and size issues can be differentiated across level (departmental, subunit, and individual) and are related to communication between managers and their colleagues. In particular, we are concerned here with exploring the following questions:

1. To what extent does the basic function of the overall organization (as defined in terms of product, overriding technology,

and market environment) influence managerial interpersonal communication behavior?

2. To what extent does the specific technical function of managers in their particular subunits appear to influence managerial communication behavior?

3. To what extent does size (departmental and subunit), separately and interactively with technology, appear to influence managerial communication behavior?

Method

Sample

The data used in the study reported here were collected from two sets of managers and their colleagues within two major subsidiaries of a large diversified corporation. The two subsidiaries differ considerably in their product and technology. One, which we have labeled "Oldline," employs a traditional, stable technology and turns out a product that has seen relatively little modification of any extreme or dramatic sort in the last several decades. It manufactures a standard, heavy-duty piece of equipment that has a fairly predictable demand in a market condition where competition generally is not marked or influenced by large shifts or developments of technological nature. In contrast, the other subsidiary, which we have called "Avtech," is concerned with sophisticated, precision-oriented technology and products that are continually evolving. The organization operates in a market environment that is relatively dynamic and somewhat unpredictable.

The procedure for collecting data was the same in both companies. Communication audit questionnaire packets were distributed to a total of 117 managers attending short management training seminars. As indicated in Chapter 2, these packets include 10 questionnaires for colleagues and a self-report focal person questionnaire to be filled out by the participating manager.

Technology Assessment

As indicated earlier, at a macro organizational level, Oldine can be described as a more traditional, stable technology organization, op-

erating in a more stable, predictable market environment than Avtech. This characterization is based on descriptive material provided
by the corporation and subsequent discussions with corporate officials
that led to the judgment that this distinction roughly captured the basic
overriding difference between the two companies.

As a more immediate measure of technology, data were collected
concerning the primary functions of the focal persons' particular
departments or divisions (e.g., engineering, accounting, marketing).
This information was interpreted in terms of the technology demands
such functions placed on the focal person at that level. Unfortunately,
differences in specific task assignments of individual focal persons and
colleagues within particular departments were not available.

Size

The two companies differ in terms of overall size as measured by
number of full-time employees, which is a potential confounding
influence when attempting to investigate the interrelationships among
the various size and technology variables. The question is: What is it
about Oldline versus Avtech that makes a difference of consequence? Is
it the distinction between the technical thrusts of the organizations, or is
it their differences in size, or both? The literature on organization size
suggests that, in the size range of the two companies being examined,
the effects of total size are small. In other words, while a difference in
organization size between a firm having 200 full-time employees and
another with 4000 employees has substantial implications for numerous aspects of the respective organizations' structures and processes, a difference between 2900 (Avtech) and 4800 (Oldline), the
observed difference here, has a minimal effect—both organizations,
Oldline and Avtech, can be considered "large."

This view is supported in part by the research of Blau and
Schoenherr (1971) whose results indicated that for organizational
characteristics such as numbers of occupational titles, numbers of local
offices, and increases took place quite rapidly with increasing agency
size but then tended to taper off for agencies with more 1000. This is
not to say that huge differences in size at the 1000 plus level are not
significant, say from 2000 employees to 10,000, but we would suggest
that the primary difference between the two "large" organizations
considered here concerns their technology and products. Thus, we

found no significant differences in the size of Oldline's and Avtech's department and work groups. They also had a fairly similar distribution of personnel across functions except for production.

Beyond the Oldline–Avtech difference in overall size, three other measures of size were obtained for each focal person: the size of the department or division; the size of the work group (the group in which the focal person and others at the same level report to the same superior); and the number of people reporting directly to the focal person.

Assessment of Communication Style, Credibility, and Outcomes

While peers, superiors, and subordinates completed colleague questionnaires on each focal person, the present analyses dealt only with subordinate responses. In the results reported here concerning focal person communication style, credibility, and outcomes, the average score across subordinate colleagues for a given focal person was calculated initially and then utilized in the statistical tests.

Analyses

The primary objective was to explore the relationships between technology, size, and communication behavior. Our aim was to test the extent to which size and technology had relevance to the general research model referred to earlier.

Incorporating the size variables into the communication model presented no methodological difficulties, as the variables were measured on an interval scale (actual number of individuals in the focal person's work group, departmental, etc.). However, technology was a categorical dichotomy—Oldline's traditional technology contrasted with Avtech's modern technology. Focal persons were located in different departments or divisions engaged in the functions of production, purchasing, research and development, sales, marketing, advertising or public relations, engineering design, client service, finance–accounting, personnel training, or other. These nominal measures could not be directly entered into the communication model. To overcome this methodological problem, the categorical measure of organizational technology was scored as 0 or 1 (traditional technology = 0; modern technology = 1). The measures of primary function were subjected to nominal decomposition (Lyons, 1971). A dummy variable was created for each functional category, and the focal person was assigned a 1 if he or she identified it as the primary function of his or her department or division and an 0 if not. (The categories "general administration" and "other" were omitted because of a small N in the case of the former and the lack of explanatory value in the latter.) This made it possible to correlate technology with the 11 communication model variables and size of two levels, organizational and departmental.

Results

Tables 6.1 and 6.2 display the intercorrelations of subordinate ratings among the 11 variables in the formal communication model for Avtech and Oldline. As can be seen, of the three outcomes variables, satisfaction with focal person and role clarity have the strongest correlations with the communication style and credibility variables though most of the correlations for job satisfaction were also significant. Intercorrelations among the five communication styles are generally moderate to low.

Table 6.3 shows the intercorrelations among size, technology, age, and education variables. Larger work groups were found in larger departments. The span of control (number of people reporting to the focal person) was also positively related to these other size measures. Larger units existed in production and engineering. Not surprisingly, age and education showed no strong relationships with the other variables.

Technology and Communication

Table 6.4 shows how organizational and biographical variables differed between Oldline and Avtech.[1] As can be seen from this table,

---

[1]Since the items in this section of the questionnaire sometimes yielded responses that were not interval, median and proportions tests of differences were utilized where t tests were inappropriate.

TABLE 6.1

Avtech Correlation Matrix: Intercorrelations of Subordinate Ratings of Focal Person's Communication Style, Credibility, and Outcomes[a]

	Careful transmitter	Open and two-way	Frank	Careful listener	Informal	Trust-worthy	Informative	Dynamic	Satisfaction with focal person	Role clarity	Job satisfaction
Communication style											
Careful transmitter											
Open and two-way	.52										
Frank	.47	.63									
Careful listener	.08	.11	-.12								
Informal	.41	.56	.51	.14							
Credibility											
Trustworthy	.46	.46	.17	.20	.51						
Informative	.38	.37	.24	.32	.28	.43					
Dynamic	.16	.33	.28	.10	.29	.27	.49				
Outcomes											
Satisfaction with focal person	.40	.43	.37	.29	.50	.53	.47	.09			
Role clarity	.45	.35	.27	.44	.43	.32	.57	.49	.44		
Job satisfaction	.28	.23	.27	.15	.39	.32	.07	.03	.51	.18	

[a]$N = 60$; coefficients greater than .07 are significant at the .05 level.

TABLE 6.2

Oldline Correlation Matrix: Intercorrelations of Subordinate Ratings of Focal Person's Communication Style, Credibility, and Outcomes[a]

	Careful transmitter	Open and two-way	Frank	Careful listener	Informal	Trust-worthy	Informative	Dynamic	Role clarity	Satisfaction with focal person	Job satisfaction
Communication style											
Careful transmitter											
Open and two-way	.53										
Frank	.46	.55									
Careful listener	.30	.47	.30								
Informal	.33	.31	.40	.37							
Credibility											
Trustworthy	.37	.49	.27	.35	.52						
Informative	.35	.60	.49	.23	.22	.59					
Dynamic	.29	.29	.40	.04	-.06	.31	.43				
Outcomes											
Role clarity	.35	.54	.52	.60	.32	.37	.41	.30			
Satisfaction with focal person	.45	.52	.45	.53	.43	.51	.55	.14	.63		
Job satisfaction	.05	.34	.31	.41	.17	.23	.25	.27	.41	.52	

[a]$N = 54$; coefficients greater than .06 are significant at the .05 level.

133

TABLE 6.3

Correlation Matrix: Intercorrelations of Size, Technology, and Age–Education Variables[a]

	Department size	Work group size	Number of people reporting to focal person	Modern vs. traditional	Production[c]	Purchasing
Department size	—					
Work group size	.25	—				
Number of people reporting	.35	.25	—			
Modern versus traditional[b]	.12	−.17	−.04	—		
Production[c]	.34	.06	.23	.30	—	
Purchasing[c]	−.16	−.07	−.27	.17	−.13	—
Research and development[c]	−.01	−.01	.11	−.04	−.10	−.10
Sales[c]	−.06	−.03	−.07	−.16	−.12	−.11
Engineering[c]	.33	.19	.21	−.04	−.14	−.13
Client service[c]	−.06	.09	.00	.12	−.05	−.04
Finance–accounting[c]	.06	.03	−.03	−.01	−.11	−.11
Personnel–training[c]	−.13	−.05	.04	−.05	−.08	−.07
Focal manager's age	−.07	−.06	.03	−.34	−.02	.07
Focal manager's education	.08	.14	.02	−.13	−.16	−.23

[a]$N = 114$; coefficients greater than .14 are significant at the .05 level.

[b]0 = Oldline company, traditional technology; 1 = Avtech Company, modern technology.

[c]The variables were coded dichotomously; e.g., 0 = nonproduction, 1 = production.

the sample of employees in Oldline was somewhat older, had more years of service in the company, and had more formal education. Although these particular biographical differences were statistically significant, their absolute differences seemed of little practical import to the issues of concern in this chapter.

Most important from a communication perspective, the size of departments and work groups as well as the distribution of personnel across functions were similar to both companies. This pattern leaves

Research and development	Sales	Engineering	Client services	Finance– accounting	Personnel– training	Focal manager's age	Focal manager's education
—							
−.09	—						
−.11	−.12	—					
−.03	−.04	−.05	—				
−.09	−.10	−.12	−.04	—			
−.06	−.07	−.08	−.02	−.06	—		
−.03	.19	−.16	−.13	−.10	−.03	—	
.15	−.12	.24	−.04	.12	.07	−.21	—

the core technology distinction between the companies as the central issue of concern.

Table 6.5 displays the mean scores of subordinate ratings of focal managers in the two companies on measures of communication style, credibility, and outcomes. Oldline managers received more favorable ratings overall. In particular, they were rated significantly higher as being careful transmitters, open and two-way in their communication style, frank, and careful listeners. Role clarity, satisfaction with focal person, and job satisfaction ratings were also higher in Oldline.

The results for role clarity support the view that traditional technology is likely to be more certain, less complex, and therefore likely to

TABLE 6.4
Summary Profile of Biographical Variables, Organizations Size Measures, and Technology[a]

Part A: Biographical Variables

Variable	Oldline[c] (N = 57) Median[b]	Avtech[c] (N = 60) Median[b]	U	N	Probability
Focal person's years of service	4.5 (12 years)	3.5 (7 years)	1225.5	−2.27	.02
Focal person's age	5.4 (44 years)	4.1 (37 years)	889.5	−4.21	.00
Focal person's education	10.2 (4-year degree +)	9.4 (3 years college +)	1332.0	−1.65	.09
Median age of focal person's colleague group	5.2 (43 years)	4.2 (38 years)	660.0	−5.45	.00
Median education of focal person's colleague group	9.2 (3 years college +)	8.8 (2 years college +)	1248.0	−2.11	.03
Focal's response: levels below you in this organization	4.8	4.1	906.5	−1.13	.25

Part B: Size

Variable	Oldline Mean	Avtech Mean	t value	Oldline SD	Avtech SD
Focal's response: number of people in your department	38.8	49.1	−1.56	34.3	35.8
Focal's response: number of people in your work group	23.7	15.7	1.49	31.2	26.1
	Oldline Median	Avtech Median	U	N	Probability
Focal's response: number of people reporting to you	2.2 (8 persons)	2.1 (5 persons)	1431.0	−.48	.63

Part C: Technology
Percentages

Focal person's department function	Oldline	Avtech	Z	Probability
Production	2	22	-3.46	.00
Purchasing	6	17	-1.84	.07
Research and development	10	7	.55	.58
Sales	16	5	1.85	.07
Engineering	16	12	.59	.56
Client service	0	3	1.34	.19
General administration	0	0	0	1.0
Finance–accounting	10	9	.17	.87
Personnel–training	6	3	.74	.46
Other	34	21	1.51	.14

[a]Differences between the two companies were assessed by the statistical technique appropriate to the level of measurement. Interval scales were subjected to a standard difference of means t test. Ordinal scales were subjected to a difference in medians Mann–Whitney U test. Nominal measures were evaluated with a difference in proportions test.

[b]Medium scores from items were used in the analysis. Response choices to some items were used in the analysis. Response choices to some items were in terms of 4–5-year blocks of time. For these items, approximate equivalent values in years are provided for ease of interpretation.

[c]Oldline = traditional technology organization; Avtech = modern technology.

137

TABLE 6.5

Means of Subordinate Group Scores of Focal Persons' Communication Styles, Credibility, and Outcomes and Their Differences between Companies

Variable	Mean[a]			SD	
	Oldline ($N = 57$ groups)	Avtech ($N = 60$ groups)	t value	Oldline	Avtech
Communication style					
Careful transmitter	6.5	5.9	6.03	1.3	1.4
Open and two-way	6.4	6.0	4.74**	1.3	1.4
Frank	6.7	6.5	2.16*	1.3	1.3
Careful listener	7.4	7.2	2.85*	1.2	1.4
Informal	6.6	6.5	.45	1.6	1.7
Credibility					
Trustworthy	7.3	7.3	.79	1.3	1.4
Informative	7.6	7.5	1.28	1.2	1.3
Dynamic	7.1	7.1	1.04	1.3	1.2
Outcomes					
Role clarity	7.3	7.0	3.66**	1.3	1.3
Satisfaction with focal person	6.7	6.4	3.67**	1.4	1.4
Job satisfaction	6.6	6.3	3.06**	1.7	1.7

[a]As in all data presentations, the potential range of scores is from 1 to 9 after transformations as described in Chapter 2.
*$p < .05$.
**$p < .01$.

permit relatively permanent and stable role responsibilities. On the other hand, Avtech with its modern technology was more likely to remain in a state of flux. It was required to be responsive to changing products and technical innovations and as a consequence was in a situation where roles would be less clear. Avtech's needs for more effective managerial communication behavior is probably due to the fact that in Oldline job definition and role responsibilities are provided to a considerable extent by the job itself and less so by colleagues in the immediate work setting.

Correlations between technology and size, on the one hand, and communication style, credibility, and outcomes, on the other, were also examined.[2] Only two relationships were statistically significant at $p <$ .05. Open and two-way and careful transmitter were negatively related ($-.15$ and $-.18$, respectively) with organizational technology (where modern technology was coded 1 and traditional technology was coded 0). Thus, being open and two-way in communication and a careful transmitter were associated with traditional organizational technology setting.

Size and Communication

Correlations were also calculated for each of the four measures of size with the communication style variables, and they were generally negative, as might be expected. That is, an increase in the size of the work units and larger units (divisions, etc.) makes it more difficult to have time for effective one-on-one communication and to come across as a careful transmitter, open and two-way, frank, a careful listener, and informal. However, none of the correlations with size was significant. Hence, while the direction of the correlations was consistent with previous research, the lack of significance was not congruent with findings reported elsewhere (Blau, 1968; Roberts & O'Reilly, 1974a; Thomas & Fink, 1963). For the credibility and outcomes measures, correlations with the four measures of size were also nonsignificant except for dynamic, which was significantly correlated (.14) with organization size.

---

[2]As noted earlier, the creation of dummy variables for technology and for the eight departments made it possible to treat departmental differences in function and organizational technology as sources of variance.

Impact of Technology and Size on the Communication Model

To summarize the interactions between variables and to see how well the formal model might describe the linkages, a path analysis was performed. The size and technology variables were posited as prior contraints that in turn influence managerial communication style, credibility, and outcomes.

The path analysis was performed through a series of regression equations. Each of the dependent measures (role clarity, satisfaction with focal person, and job satisfaction) were regressed in a hierarchical fahion against the intervening, communication, and size and technology ariables. Beta coefficients between these dependent measures and the intervening variables therefore reflect the remaining variables (communication, size, and technology) acting through the intervening variables (trustworthy, informative, dynamic). Similarly, each of the intervening variables was regressed against the communication and the size and technology variables in a hierarchical fashion and resulting beta coefficients noted. As the final stage, each of the communication variables was regressed against the size and technology variables. The level of variance explained (noted in parentheses with the variables in the path model shown in Figure 6.1) reflects values for that variable acting as a dependent measure against the preceding variables indicated by the direction of the arrow. In performing the various steps of the analysis, paths having coefficients less than .15 were eliminated from the model and the remaining coefficients were recalculated.

As seen in Figure 6.1, organizational technology (traditional versus modern) was negatively linked to the tendency to be careful as a transmitter and listener. This would suggest that, as we move from traditional to modern technology in our two samples, managers are rated less highly in these areas of communication behavior. Production and sales also emerge as negative predictors of careful listener and as positive predictors of informal. These relationships held while controlling for basic technology of the organization, suggesting that for certain functional areas the specific function performed by the manager overrides the larger organizational function.

Department size negatively predicts open and two-way communication. None of the other size measures was significant.

Among the intervening variables, trustworthiness is influenced by open and two-way, informal, and frank, whereas informativeness appears to be best predicted by open and two-way and careful listener.

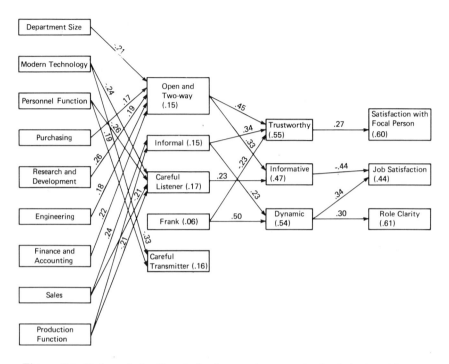

Figure 6.1. Path analysis: Size, technology, and communication behavior. All path coefficients shown here are significant at the .05 level. The numbers in parentheses within the boxes are the obtained R^2 values.

Dynamism is influenced positively by frankness and informality of style.

Finally, among the three outcomes, satisfaction with focal person and role clarity are best explained by the model (R^2 = .60 and .61, respectively), followed by job satisfaction (R^2 = .44). Thus, communication behavior appears to relate more directly to satisfaction with the communicator and perceptions of role clarity as compared to a subordinate's own sense of overall satisfaction with his or her own work.

Conclusion

This present chapter provides only tentative evidence concerning the relationships between organizational technology, organizational size dimensions, and interpersonal communications. However, among other things, the patterns suggest that technology may be of greater importance than size in understanding communication behavior.

The overall technical function of the organization appears to have a significant independent effect on the communication styles of managers, and at the same time, the specific technology or function of a manager may in some cases also impact that manager's communication style, independent of the basic production function of the organization. In the path analysis, several functional measures of immediate technology revealed significant patterns. However, these variables were at best rough approximations in measuring the more immediate level technology in which these managers and their subordinates were engaged. In subsequent research, better measures of technology at the work level are required so that this dimension can be examined more closely in relation to communication behavior.

In general terms, it might be concluded that effective communication is more difficult to achieve in high-technology settings (as compared to traditional technology organizations), since the nature of the work is relatively less predictable and routine and since expertise is likely to be more widely disbursed. Hence, communication skills training would be particularly important in high-technology organizations.

It appears from the present analysis that size per se was not a significant factor in a manager's communication style. This result obtained no matter at what level size was measured, and it reflects the findings reported in Chapter 5, which also failed to indicate significant relationships between size and communication variables.

7

The Work Setting as
an Information Environment

In previous chapters, we examined technology, size, and interpersonal distance in relation to managerial communication behavior as it impacts on colleagues. In the present chapter, we extend our focus to consider the work group setting as an information environment. We use this perspective to examine the perceived value and importance of the focal person as an information source. We also examine the perceptions of managerial communication style, credibility, satisfaction, and role clarity in relation to characteristics of the work group setting as an information environment.

The Work Group Setting as an
Information Environment

The basis for viewing the task or work group setting as an information environment has roots in a number of disciplines, including organizational behavior, speech communication, management science, psychology, as well as computer–information systems. Some of the early psychological theories of human behavior (Bruner, Goodnow, & Austin, 1956; Tolman, 1932; Tolman & Brunswick, 1935) helped to shape the view of individuals as complex information processing systems who have severe cognitive limits in their ability to process information for decision making in organizational contexts (March & Simon, 1958; Newell, Shaw, & Simon, 1958; Simon, 1947, 1955, 1956). Related to this perspective is research on personality and cognitive style that focuses on how and why people select, perceive, and combine information as a basis for action (e.g., Festinger, 1957; McKenney, 1971; Schroder, Driver, & Streufert, 1967). Extending these ideas beyond the individual level to subunits, the organization, and its environment, it can be argued that organizational decision making will depend on information processing styles, which in turn vary considerably across differing organizational contexts as a function of the problem and of the task demands of the work environment.

Research on management information systems (MIS), computers, and management science has also been concerned with an information processing perspective on the work environment, particularly in terms of how information can be efficiently captured, processed, displayed, and distributed to appropriate organizational units and individuals for monitoring and decision-making purposes (e.g., Huysmans, 1970; Mason & Mitroff, 1973; Mock, 1973). While studies in this area have varied widely in their focus, a common thread is the issue of information management for organizations.

At a more operational level, viewing the work context as an information environment forces us to focus more explicitly on what elements in a person's information environment take on the most meaning for that person (i.e., how and why he or she selects, interprets, and values certain information sources) and how the individual combines and utilizes such information as a guide to action. Moving beyond the individual level to groups and the organizational–task setting, similar questions emerge. Research by Katz and Tushman (1979), for example, points out important linkages between communication patterns for transferring administrative and problem solving information, task characteristics, and project performance of work groups in R&D settings. Other research reinforces the usefulness of concentrating on the task as an information environment and on the relationships between sources, types, and reliability of information and job satisfaction in different organizational settings (Greller & Herold, 1975; Hanser & Muchinsky, 1978).

In short, conceiving occupational settings as information environ-ments has considerable theoretical as well as empirical support as a

way of understanding how people accomplish work and their satisfaction with it. In the present chapter, these ideas are examined further
in relation to styles of communication, task characteristics of the work
setting, and perceptions of the importance of a focal person as an
information source for getting work done in the work group setting.

Method

Sample

The data reported here were collected at two military bases and in a
social service agency setting. For the two military samples, the focal
persons were identified by a senior officer at each base and were asked
to participate in the survey. The response rate of focal persons was 80%
at one base and 70% at the other. In the social service sample, the focal
persons completed the questionnaires while attending a training
course. All agreed to participate. Table 7.1 provides a summary profile
of focal persons and their subordinates.

Comparisons between the samples indicated that focal persons and
their subordinates at Base I tended to be somewhat younger and have
more years of formal education than those in the other samples. In
addition, they had fewer years of service. Not surprisingly, the large
majority of respondents in the two military bases were male, while in
the social service setting the majority were female. The number of
persons reporting to the focal person was similar across organizations.

Of greatest interest to us in the discussion that follows are potential
differences between the military versus nonmilitary organizational
setting. Given the great similarity in organizational structure, mission,
and personnel in the two bases as compared to the social service
sample, responses for the two military samples have been combined.

Data

A questionnaire containing the communication styles survey items as
well as supplemental items that probed aspects of the focal person's
work situation was assembled (see Appendix 7.A, pp. 156–158). Fifteen

TABLE 7.1
Summary Profile of Biographical and Organizational Variables

Variables	Military base I		Military base II		Social service sample	
	Focal persons (N = 38)	Subordinates (N = 153)	Focal persons (N = 31)	Subordinates (N = 149)	Focal persons (N = 26)	Subordinates (N = 142)
Average age (years)	31	27	38	32	34	32
Sex						
Percentage male	100	98	97	85	31	20
Percentage female	0	2	3	15	69	80
Median education level (years)	17	16.5	16	13.5	16	16
Median years of service	6		15		12	
Number of people reporting to focal person (average for each organization)	8		5		6	

items in the first part of the supplement focused on dimensions of a person's job (need for teamwork, routineness, information, feedback from work, etc.). Most of these items were taken from task input and within-system scales in a questionnaire previously developed by Bass, Farrow, Valenzi, and Solomon (1975). Other items in this section probed in more depth the information–communication characteristics of the focal person (Items 19–28). Items included in this supplement are shown in Appendix 7.A.

Questionnaires were completed by focal persons as well as their colleagues at work (including all their subordinates, their supervisor(s), and peers), who responded to the set of questions in terms of how they viewed the focal person and the work situation. The completed questionnaires were forwarded directly to the research team for analysis. Participating focal persons subsequently received the communication audit profile information in the feedback format described in Chapter 2.

Development of Task and Information Environment Scales

For the military and social service samples, the supplemental work-related items of the questionnaire were factor analyzed as a way of identifying basic dimensions of the task and information environment as well as characteristics of the focal person as an information source. Principal components factor analysis (with varimax rotation) was utilized, with the number of factors being determined by factors possessing an eigenvalue greater than 1.0. Items having loadings greater than .50 on a factor were identified in developing each scale. Seven scales were derived with adequate internal consistency reliability. A summary description of the scales is provided in Table 7.2. Mean scores and the internal consistency reliability for each scale in the military and social service settings are shown in Table 7.3.

The pattern of item loadings for the four task environment scales replicated the scales reported by Bass et al. (1975) and pertain to the characteristics and demands of the work context (teamwork require-ments, complexity, routineness of task, and extent to which the job context provides task feedback). The remaining scales relate to the usefulness and importance of the focal person as an information source, for decision making, and for doing the job.

TABLE 7.2
Scales Dealing with Task Environment and Focal Person as an
Information Source

Scale	Definition	Item number[a]
Task environment		
Teamwork	Extent members of unit work together, depend on each other to get work done	2, 6, 10, 13
Complexity	Extent one's work involves complex analysis, complex work	4, 8, 15
Task feedback	Extent one knows when one is doing a good job	3, 9
Routineness	Extent one's work is routine	7, 12
Focal person as an information source		
Focal person information useful	Extent of satisfaction with the quality, timeliness, and quantity of information from the focal person	16, 17, 18
Focal person information importance	Extent focal person is an important information source for doing the job	25, 27, 28
Decision-making information	Importance of focal person information for formal decision making	20, 22, 24

[a]The items forming the task environment scales and those pertaining to focal person as an information source are in the supplemental questionnaire shown in Appendix 7.A. The numbers in the above column labeled "Item number" indicate which items in the questionnaire form each scale.

Results

As suggested in previous research (e.g., Katz & Tushman, 1979), the demands of the task environment influence the choice and relative value of information and communication behavior. This issue is considered more specifically here in terms of the relationship between subordinates' perceptions of their task environment, the importance of information from the focal person for getting work done, communication style and credibility of the focal person, and subordinate role clarity and satisfaction.

TABLE 7.3
Task and Information Source Scales (Based on Subordinate Responses)

Scale name	Number of items[c]	Military sample[a]			Social service sample[b]		
		Mean	SD	Reliability	Mean	SD	Reliability
Teamwork	4	17.9	2.1	.68	14.5	3.2	.57
Complexity	3	10.2	3.0	.68	8.8	2.9	.47
Feedback	2	8.4	1.2	.35	7.4	1.8	.24
Routineness	2	5.9	2.1	.76	6.1	2.2	.26
Focal person information useful	3	10.1	3.6	.86	7.6	4.5	.98
Focal person information importance	3	8.6	3.3	.67	6.3	3.9	.93
Decision-making information	3	6.5	2.4	.52	5.4	3.1	.70

[a]Military sample = 69 groups.

[b]Social service sample = 26 groups.

[c]Each item had a 5-point scale. Thus, the range for a 4-item scale is 4–20. See Apendix 7.A for specific items and response categories.

Task Environment

Scales 1–4 in Table 7.4 provide subordinate ratings of the task environment in the military and social service settings. For both organizations, the intercorrelations were generally relatively low, indicating the empirical independence of each factor in these two work settings. While the pattern of correlations for both organizations was similar in most instances, in two cases the direction of the correlations was different (complexity with feedback and complexity with routineness). In the social service setting, greater complexity was associated with less feedback (−.17) and less routineness (−.11), whereas in the military organization, the relationship was reversed (.05 and .14, respectively). However, none of the correlations was significant.

Focal Person as an Information Source

Scales 5–7 in Table 7.4 focus on the importance, usefulness, and decision-making value of the information coming from the focal person, as seen by subordinates. As shown in the lower right-hand portion of the table, these variables all quite highly and significantly correlated for both samples. This pattern makes sense intuitively in that information that is important to a subordinate is more than likely to be seen as useful (in terms of timeliness, quality, and quantity) and as valuable input for decision-making purposes. Thus, all three factors, though conceptually distinct from each other, are likely to occur together across work settings.

Task Environment and Focal Person as an Information Source

Of particular interest in the pattern of correlations were the relationships between task characteristics and perceptions of the significance of the focal person as an information source for getting the work done. Not surprisingly, task feedback (knowing if one is doing a good job) had the strongest relationship to the three measures of focal person as an information source.

TABLE 7.4
Correlation Matrix: Task Characteristics of Focal Person's Work Unit and Focal Person as an Information Source (as Seen by Subordinates)[a]

Scale	2	3	4	5	6	7
Task environment						
1. Teamwork	.13, .12	.02, .07	.02, .15	.14, −.25	.05, −.28	.21, .19
2. Complexity		.05, −.17	.14, −.11	.17, −.14	−.13, .00	.03, .03
3. Feedback			.19, .11	**.46, .45**[b]	**.43, .43**	**.34, .29**
4. Routineness				−.10, −.11	−.12, −.14	−.18, −.18
Focal person (as information source)						
5. Focal person information useful					**.58, .84**	**.49, .49**
6. Focal person information importance						**.55, .62**
7. Decision-making input						

[a]Correlations are based on mean score values for each group of subordinates for a given focal person. The first correlation is for the combined military sample, the second correlation is for the social service sample.
[b]Boldface values are significant at $p < .05$.

151

Task Environment, Focal Person as an Information Source,
Communication Style, Credibility, and Outcomes

A central concern here is whether the task environment and the focal
person as information source relate in important ways to the communication style of the focal person and to credibility as well as
satisfaction and role clarity. As a way of understanding such relationships, correlations among key variables of concern were calculated.

TASK ENVIRONMENT

Table 7.5 presents the correlations between the four task variables
and communication style, credibility, and outcomes for both organizational settings. Of the four task variables, task feedback yielded the
strongest correlations. This comes as no surprise in that subordinates
are likely to count on communication from their supervisors as the
critical determinants in how well they are performing their jobs. Thus,
all five communication style dimensions are positively correlated with
task feedback. The same largely held in both samples. As for the three
outcomes, as expected, role clarity had the largest correlation with task
feedback but was also quite strongly related to satisfaction with focal
person, suggesting that subordinates are more satisfied with their
bosses when they get feedback on how well they are doing their jobs. In
the military sample, it was also significantly related to job satisfaction.

The correlations for the other three task variables were in general
much less strong and consistent. Routineness was significantly
correlated in only 1 of 22 cases (negatively with informal in the military
setting.). Three of the correlations for teamwork with the communication, credibility, and outcome variables were significant for the
military sample (informal, informative, and satisfaction with focal
person), but none was in the case of the social service sample. Task
complexity yielded one significant correlation for the military group,
but not for the social service group.

This overall pattern thus suggests that a manager's communication
style and credibility are largely separate from teamwork demands,
routineness of task, and complexity, but that in the area of task
feedback the manager plays an important role.

TABLE 7.5
Correlation Matrix: Task Characteristics, Communication Style, Credibility, and Outcomes[a]

	Teamwork		Complexity		Feedback		Routineness	
	Military	Social service	Military	Social service	Military	Social service	Military	Social service
Communication style								
Careful transmitter	.08	-.15	-.05	-.18	**.38**	.31	-.03	.08
Open and two-way	.09	.02	.06	-.24	**.33**	**.47**	-.12	-.14
Frank	.20	-.03	.10	.12	**.41**	**.59**	-.07	.00
Careful listener	.14	-.11	-.06	-.15	**.28**	.13	-.02	-.23
Informal	**.24**	-.04	.00	-.16	**.32**	.33	-**.27**	-.04
Credibility								
Trustworthy	.15	.04	-.05	-.12	.22	.17	-.20	-.15
Informative	**.40**	-.21	.10	-.01	**.35**	**.41**	-.13	-.10
Dynamic	.23	-.03	**.29**	.13	**.27**	.29	.18	-.27
Outcomes								
Role clarity	.08	.06	.11	.21	**.46**	**.49**	.00	.13
Job satisfaction	.06	-.20	.06	.00	**.35**	.11	.16	.38
Satisfaction with focal person	**.28**	.05	.15	-.10	**.40**	.38	-.09	-.06

[a]Military sample (N = 67); social services sample (N = 23). Boldface correlations are significant at $p < .05$.

TABLE 7.6

Correlation Matrix: Focal Person as an Information Source, Communication Style, Credibility, and Outcomes[a]

	Focal person information useful		Focal person information importance		Decision-making information	
	Military	Social service	Military	Social service	Military	Social service
Communication style						
Careful transmitter	.62	.80	.56	.68	.39	.54
Open and two-way	.75	.83	.47	.75	.43	.63
Frank	.61	.70	.36	.66	.33	.54
Careful listener	.52	.77	.36	.68	.30	.63
Informal	.63	.55	.49	.47	.42	.54
Credibility						
Trustworthy	.55	.58	.45	.43	.42	.48
Informative	.61	.94	.45	.89	.36	.55
Dynamic	.41	.66	.20	.70	.07	.43
Outcomes						
Role clarity	.70	.62	.46	.54	.47	.50
Job satisfaction	.38	.28	.33	.18	.21	.18
Satisfaction with focal person	.80	.92	.59	.85	.47	.64

[a]Military sample ($N = 67$); social service sample ($N = 23$). All correlations are significant *except* those in italics.

FOCAL PERSON AS AN INFORMATION SOURCE

The correlations between the three measures of focal person as information source and communication style, credibility, and outcomes are shown in Table 7.6. Almost all correlation coefficients were significant and strongly positive in both samples. Thus, being seen as a careful transmitter, open and two-way, frank, a careful listener, and informal was significantly related to providing useful and important information and being seen as important input for decision making. Similar relationships appeared for the credibility measures and the three measures of focal person as information source, although in two instances the correlations with dynamic were not significant. Among the outcomes, not surprisingly, the strongest relationships were between satisfaction with focal person and the three measures of focal person as information source. Next in importance were the relationships with role clarity, while for job satisfaction, four out of six correlations were not significant. Job satisfaction has been shown in other research to include several elements, such as satisfaction with the work itself, pay and promotions, and co-workers, as well as satisfaction with supervision (e.g., Cook, Hepworth, Well, & Warr, 1981; Smith *et al.*, 1969). As noted in Chapter 2, our general measure of job satisfaction did not tap all these subelements. Hence, it is understandable that the correlations were lower for this variable.

It might be noted that, among the three measures of focal person as information source, usefulness of focal person information (in terms of quality, timeliness, and quantity received) consistently had the strongest correlations with communication style, credibility, and outcomes. Thus, being a careful transmitter, open and two-way, frank, a careful listener, and informal in communication with subordinates is particularly strongly associated with perceptions of the timeliness, quality, and quantity of information received from the focal person. The relationships between information usefulness and credibility (especially informativeness), and satisfaction with focal person were similarly strong.

Conclusion

The findings in this chapter indicate some rather consistent relationships between task, focal person as information source, and communication style, credibility, and outcomes. In general, the strong correlations between communication style, credibility, and outcomes on the one hand and the three measures of focal person as information source and the task dimension of feedback support the utility of viewing the work setting as an information environment. The observed importance of the focal person (supervisor) in this information environment is consistent with results from other research that has studied the work context as an information environment. For example, Hanser and Muchinsky (1978) found that supervision was the most reliable information source concerning the job, compared with the task itself, co-workers, the formal organization, and personal thoughts and feelings as sources of information.

Still to be developed, however, is a more detailed picture of what specific communication styles are best suited for and contribute to high levels of job performance in different kinds of work settings. Moreover, it is not clear to what extent managers are likely to modify their communication styles depending on the characteristics of the task environment. These important issues need further elaboration under more controlled conditions. However, the results reported here suggest that further research in this direction is warranted.

Appendix 7.A: Supplemental Questionnaire—Part WS: Your Work Situation

The statements in this part describe your work situation. Some are mainly about your own particular job. Some are mainly about your immediate work group, the group which includes yourself, others, and the boss to whom you all report. For items 1–15, in the blank space next to each statement write the number which best describes how true or false each statement is or how strongly you agree or disagree with it. The numbers represent the following:

        5 = Definitely True, or Strongly Agree
        4 = Mostly True, or Generally Agree
        3 = Neither True nor False, or Neither Agree nor Disagree
        2 = Mostly False, or Generally Disagree
        1 = Definitely False, or Strongly Disagree
        7 = Does Not Apply

EXAMPLE:
____4____ Rules and regulations are strictly enforced in your work group.
           (The respondent's "4" next to the statement indicates that the respondent generally agrees that the statement is mostly true about the work group.)

_____ 1. There is more than one right way to do your job.
_____ 2. To do their jobs properly, members of your work group must work closely together.
_____ 3. It is clear to you what someone in your job should get done.
_____ 4. In your job, you analyze complex information or data.
_____ 5. There are "standard operating procedures" for your job.
_____ 6. People in your work group depend upon work done by other people in the work group to get their own jobs done.
_____ 7. Your daily work is taken up by routine activities.

—————— 8. Your work is complicated.

—————— 9. You are told how good or bad your work is.

—————— 10. Members of your group work together as a team.

—————— 11. There are several ways you could do your job.

—————— 12. Only a small part of your work is routine.

—————— 13. Members of your work group have little need to work with each other.

—————— 14. You never know for sure if you are doing a good job.

—————— 15. Compared to most others in your organization, you must understand more about the use of data processing equipment or other complex machinery.

—————— 16. Overall, how satisfied are you with the quality of information you receive from the focal person?

Use scale below for items 16–18.

5 = extremely satisfied
4 = very satisfied
3 = satisfied
2 = only slightly satisfied
1 = not satisfied
7 = does not apply

—————— 17. Overall, how satisfied are you with the timeliness of information you receive from the focal person?

—————— 18. Overall, how satisfied are you with the quantity of information you receive from the focal person?

. . . .

—————— 19. The focal person initiates communications with you.

Use scale below for items 19–23.

5 = always
4 = frequently if not always
3 = quite often
2 = sometimes
1 = once in a while
0 = never
7 = does not apply

—————— 20. Generally speaking, how frequently is the information you need for decision making obtained from the focal person?

—————— 21. Your communication with the focal person is informal and impromptu.

—————— 22. Communications you have with the focal person occur at scheduled occasions. (Preplanned appointments or meetings)

_____ 23. The focal person is accessible to you when you want to contact him or her.

. . . .

_____ 24. Generally speaking, how *important* or valuable do you find the information from the focal person for decision making in your work?

_____ 25. Compared with others with whom you work, how important is the focal person to you as an information source within the organization?

_____ 26. How important are *you* to the focal person as an information source on matters regarding how you do your own job?

_____ 27. How important is the focal person to you as an information source on matters regarding how you do your own job?

_____ 28. How important is the focal person in providing a clear understanding of the overall responsibilities that go with the position you occupy?

Use scale below for items 24–28.

5 = extremely important
4 = very important
3 = important
2 = only slightly important
1 = not important
7 = does not apply

Communication,
Managerial Style, and Success

As already noted in Chapter 1, there is a considerable degree of overlap in conceptualizing communication and leadership behavior. Nevertheless, there is little empirical research that examines relationships between them.

In this chapter, we will first look at how communication and leadership behavior are intertwined. From empirical results, we will attempt to specify the communication styles that tend to cluster with different leadership styles. Second, we will examine the extent to which a manager's communication style contributes to his or her success as a manager, measured by a salary grade attained beyond predictions.

Communication Behavior and Leadership

In this section, we will present results obtained in examining how communication patterns of focal persons relate to their leadership or managerial styles.

Measuring Leadership Style

Based on a series of questionnaire surveys of subordinates who described the behavior of thier superiors, Bass, Valenzi, Farrow, and Solomon (1975) used scores on 72 items of leadership behavior to generate five factors: direction, negotiation, consultation, participation, and delegation. The stylistic factors were described as follows:

> *Direction:* The directive manager tells his subordinates what to do and how to do it. He initiates actions. He tells subordinates what is expected of them. He sets deadlines for the completion of work by his subordinates. He specifies definite standards of performance expected from his subordinates. He rules firmly and maintains uniform ways of doing things. He schedules what work his subordinates will do and tells them to follow standard rules and regulations. He sees to it that subordinates are working to capacity and reassigns tasks to balance the workload.

> *Negotiation:* The negotiative manager does personal favors for those who work for him. He is opportunistic and changes his behavior to fit the occasion. He promises rewards if subordinates follow his opinions. He times the release of information for when it will do him the most good. He makes political alliances with superiors and subordinates. He maintains social distance: remains aloof, detached, and un-involved with subordinates. He bends rules to get the job done. He encourages subordinates to compete with each other. He "sells" his decisions to his subordinates.

> *Consultation:* The decisions the consultative leader makes reflect the fact that he has discussed matters with his subordinates before he decides. He does not make final decisions unless he hears first what his subordinates think about the matter. He makes the final decisions but only after obtaining his subordinates' opinions. Before he makes up his mind, he explains the problem to his subordinates to get their opinions. He does not act on important matters before first hearing subordinates' ideas. He talks things over first with subordinates, then decides what action to take.

> *Participation:* The participative leader and his subordinates analyze problems to reach consensual decisions. His subordinates have as much responsibility for final decisions as he does. Decisions are made by the group, not by him alone. Decisions that affect the work group are made in joint decision making con-ferences between himself and his subordinates. His subordinates participate as equals in decision making.

> *Delegation:* He gives suggestions but leaves group members free to follow their own courses. He permits subordinates to make their own decisions. Subordinates decide what to do and how to do it after he indicates that a problem exists. He leaves matters in the hands of his subordinates.

Bass *et al.* (1975) noted that direction and negotiation were empirically correlated for many samples of managers. Both were aspects of *initiation of structure*. Consultation, participation, and negotiation were also intercorrelated as elements of *consideration*. Nevertheless, response allocation analyses showed that the five factors were conceptually independent. Delegation is very different than consultation, although the same managers tend to do both or to do neither.

As can be seen, much of each factor involves different ways of communicating with subordinates. Hence, the results of correlating communication style scores with these five leadership factor scores were not unexpected. Rather, they confirmed the extent to which much of leadership behavior is covered by communication style.

Sample

Necessary data for analysis were obtained from 71 social service professionals and their 28 superiors. The 71 subordinate colleagues described the communication styles, credibility, and outcomes for their 28 superiors as focal persons. They also completed the Management Styles Survey (Bass, 1976), which yielded the five factor scores about the leadership behavior of the focal persons (their supervisors). Self-evaluations were also obtained from the 28 superiors (focal persons) about their communication patterns and leadership behavior.

Results

Table 8.1 shows the correlations for the 71 subordinates describing the leadership and the communication behavior of their superiors. All subordinates describing the same focal person were grouped, and the mean communication and leadership behavior obtained for each person was the basis for the correlations reported in Table 8.1. Table 8.2 shows how the 28 focal persons described themselves on corresponding questionnaires.

Table 8.1 answers the question: When subordinates describe their superiors' leadership behavior, are they also to some extent describing their superiors' communication behavior? Table 8.2 answers the question: When focal persons describe how they think they lead are they at the same time describing how they communicate? As can be seen, clearly distinct patterns emerge.

For subordinates, consultative, participative, or delegative leadership was strongly linked to the focal person's communication styles,

TABLE 8.1
Relations between Communication Styles and Management Styles as Seen by Seventy-One Subordinates of Twenty-Eight Focal Persons[a]

	Directive	Negotiative	Consultative	Participative	Delegative	Mean[b]	SD
Communication style							
Careful transmitter	**.37**	.08	**.63**	**.59**	**.64**	5.7	1.9
Open and two-way	**.36**	.06	**.70**	**.65**	**.61**	5.6	2.0
Frank	**.42**	.04	**.50**	**.45**	**.36**	6.0	1.9
Careful listener	.15	−.08	**.51**	**.55**	**.59**	6.8	1.7
Informal	.18	−.01	**.53**	**.55**	**.55**	6.4	2.2
Credibility							
Trustworthy	.19	−.03	**.57**	**.54**	**.57**	6.7	1.9
Informative	**.31**	−.05	**.59**	**.58**	**.63**	6.5	2.2
Dynamic	**.49**	−.08	**.38**	.25	.14	7.0	1.4
Outcomes							
Role clarity	**.36**	−.02	**.37**	**.40**	**.43**	7.1	1.5
Satisfaction with focal person	**.35**	.02	**.62**	**.64**	**.63**	6.1	2.0
Job satisfaction	.18	.10	**.29**	**.30**	**.31**	6.0	1.6
Mean	7.8	4.0	6.8	5.2	7.4		
SD	2.8	2.2	3.4	3.4	3.4		

[a]Boldface values are significant at $p < .01$.
[b]As in all data presentations, the potential range of scores is from 1 to 9.

TABLE 8.2
Relations between Self-Appraised Communication Styles and Management Styles of Twenty-Eight Focal Persons[a]

	Directive	Negotiative	Consultative	Participative	Delegative	Mean[b]	SD
Communication style							
Careful transmitter	.09	**-.38**	.04	-.09	-.09	5.6	1.2
Open and two-way	.17	-.24	.27	.19	.08	6.1	1.2
Frank	.09	-.16	-.02	-.07	-.06	5.6	1.4
Careful listener	-.15	**-.48**	-.18	-.22	-.11	7.0	1.0
Informal	-.13	**-.43**	-.07	-.10	-.10	6.0	1.4
Credibility							
Trustworthy	-.07	-.28	.10	.05	-.04	6.8	1.3
Informative	.11	-.17	.17	.21	.07	6.9	1.4
Dynamic	-.05	**-.33**	.00	-.09	-.19	6.2	1.2
Outcomes							
Role clarity	**.30**	-.13	**.39**	.24	.10	6.5	1.0
Satisfaction with focal person	-.04	-.14	.11	.20	.17	6.4	1.1
Job satisfaction	.12	-.09	.11	.17	.14	6.0	2.0
Mean	5.8	4.2	5.6	4.6	7.4		
SD	3.4	1.6	3.8	2.6	2.6		

[a]Boldface values are significant at $p < .05$.

[b]As in all data presentations, the potential range of scores is from 1 to 9.

credibility, and outcomes—with two exceptions. Dynamism correlated significantly only with directive and consultative leadership behavior (see Table 8.1). But self-appraisals by focal persons were completely different (see Table 8.2). Only one relation was significant. Self-rated consultative leadership behavior correlated .39 with self-rated role clarity. Negotiative behavior was irrelevant in the eyes of subordinates, possibly because it is less easy to discern reliably. However, the focal persons themselves saw that, if they were negotiative, they also were much less likely to be careful transmitters, careful listeners, and informal. Directiveness of the focal person, as seen by subordinates, was significantly associated with the focal person's careful transmission, open and two-way communication, and frankness, but not careful listening or informality of style. It was also associated with informativeness, dynamism, role clarity, and satisfaction with the focal person. With focal person self-appraisals (see Table 8.2), directiveness was independent of self-rated style and credibility of the focal person, and related significantly only to the focal person's perceptions of role clarity of their subordinates.

Communication Style and Success as a Manager

If promotion is based on merit, particularly interpersonal competence, we should expect successful managers to be seen by their colleagues as more credible, open and two-way, trustworthy, informative, as well as effective in transmitting and listening. On the other hand, if promotion is based on favorably manipulating one's superiors, then most colleagues are likely to see such rapidly rising managers as lower in most of these regards. Several empirical investigations have shown that the more rapidly promoted mangers are likely to be more pragmatic rather than idealistic or moralistic (Bass, Burger, Doktor, & Barrett, 1979; Bass & Eldridge, 1973; England & Weber, 1972). One might expect this to be reflected in the communication style scores for careful listening and transmitting. That is, as pragmatists, successful focal persons would be more likely to expend the effort to transmit and listen carefully when the occasion warranted. An idealist would be expected to be more concerned about this in all his or her interchanges.

Defining and Measuring Success as a Manager

One approach to measuring success as a manager has been to regard higher level managers as more successful than lower level managers. Promotion to higher levels or number of promotions earned is seen as an index of managerial success. Or one may choose to contrast cross-sectional samples of managers and nonmanagers. Managers are defined as organizationally successful; nonmanagers are not successful in these terms. Thus, Bray, Campbell, and Grant (1974) compared employees who started out together in terms of whether subsequently they succeeded in attaining middle-management jobs.

Managers' success is frequently measured by ratings of their performance, usually by superiors (Stogdill, 1974). Success has also been measured in terms of rate of advancement up the executive ladder. A younger person at a higher management level or with a higher salary has risen faster or at an accelerated rate. An older person at a lower management level or with a lower salary has risen more slowly or at a decelerated pace (Bass & Eldridge, 1973). Level and salary tend to correlate highly. For Esso Europe managers, Laurent (1968) found a correlation of .82. England (1976) as well as Laurent (1968) looked at managers' salary, holding constant nonachievement factors likely to influence salary, such as seniority and function. They both derived an index for each manager based on the discrepancy between actual salary and the salary forecast by seniority, function, age, and so forth. A manager was therefore seen as more successful, the more his or her actual salary was greater than predicted. Thus, in using this procedure, Farrow, Valenzi, and Bass (1981) found it possible to optimize and cross-validate prediction of salary with the following equation:

Predicted Salary = 5527.86 + 4690.74 profit/nonprofit − 2356.60 sex + 2647.30 starting salary + 461.77 years of service + 428.27 total persons in organization

That is, managers' salaries were expected to be higher if they worked for a profit-making rather than a not-for-profit organization; if they were male, not female; if they began with higher starting salaries; if they had more seniority; and if they were members of larger organizations. Further, Farrow *et al.* (1981) found that, where subordinates perceived their supervisors to be negotiative or manipulative, leadership tended to result in ineffective work unit performance ($r = -.25$). Contrarily, the more negotiative the managers, the more likely they were to earn salaries in excess of what would be expected for managers of their organization type (profit or nonprofit), sex, starting salary, years of service, and size of organization. No other leadership style was associated with such excess salaries. To the degree that compensation reflects how the managers' superiors value them, superiors see greater effectiveness in managers who are manipulative; the subordinates of the managers see otherwise.

Given these results as well as the earlier observations about the extent that accelerated managers are likely to be pragmatic rather than idealistic, we expected to obtain lower scores among our accelerated managers in openness and trustworthiness, even though we saw such style and credibility contributing to satisfaction and effectivenss.

Samples

In addition to 29 social service supervisors (one additional case) from the sample used in the preceding section, we also obtained the necessary data for 159 industrial managers and 69 military officers. The 29 social service supervisors were rated by 117 subordinates, 47 peers, and 31 superiors. The 159 industrial managers were rated by 517 subordinates, 394 peers, and 195 superiors. The 69 military officers were rated by 179 subordinates, 199 peers, and 112 superiors.[1]

Predicted Salary Grade

The following variables were entered into a stepwise regression, with focal person's salary as the dependent variable: age, sex, education, years of service, total number of persons in the organization, department population, number in work group, number reporting to focal, industrial (0) or government (1) organization, and focal person's

---

[1]The military officers were the same sample discussed in Chapter 7. The industrial managers included 114 of the 117 managers (3 cases were dropped because of missing values) considered in Chapter 6 plus an additional sample of 45 managers from another firm. The subordinate sample size for the county social service organization is larger in this analysis compared to the one in the previous section because of missing values and the fact that not all of them were given the Management Styles Survey form to complete.

starting salary. The optimal prediction equation resulting from the regressions is as follows:

Predicted Salary Grade $= 8.88 + .56$ starting grade level $+ 1.24$ years of service $+ .041$ department size$^a - .93$ sex$^b + .472$ educational level^c

^{a}Actual number of people.
^{b}2 = female; 1 = male.
^{c}14 possible levels.

A predicted salary grade was then generated for all focal managers, and the measure was compared with their actual salary. The discrepancy was then computed for each focal manager by subtracting predicted salary from actual salary.

Focal persons were seen as more successful to the extent their actual salary was higher than predicted by the structural equation and as less successful to the degree their salary was less than predicted.

Results

Table 8.3 shows the results obtained for the three samples. As in Chapter 5, we excluded an examination of role clarity and job satisfaction outcomes for peers and superiors of the focal person in the present analysis since focal persons will very likely influence their subordinates in these outcomes much more than they will peers or their own superiors.

No simple pattern or directionality emerged for the three samples. Relations seem situation specific and rater specific. The success of social service professionals was associated positively with the extent their subordinates saw them as open and two-way communicators ($r = .25$) and negatively with superiors' ratings of focal person trust-worthiness ($r = -.30$). Among industrial managers, success was most strongly related to being shown by one's superiors as a careful trans-mitter, frank, informative, and as a source of satisfactory relationships.

Among the military officers who served as focal persons, as with the social service professionals, success was associated with being seen by subordinates as open and two-way communicators. Careful listening also helped. But subordinates' perceptions of focal person dynamism and role clarity were negatively associated with focal person success.

TABLE 8.3
Correlation of Colleage Ratings of Focal Persons with Their Managerial Success

Raters:	Social service personnel			Industrial personnel			Military officers		
	Subordinates (N = 117)	Peers (N = 47)	Superiors (N = 31)	Subordinates (N = 517)	Peers (N = 394)	Superiors (N = 195)	Subordinates (N = 179)	Peers (N = 199)	Superiors (N = 112)
Communication style									
Careful transmitter	-.02	.09	-.14	-.05	.04	.20**	-.06	-.17**	-.03
Open and two-way	.25**	.18	.01	-.07	-.04	.08	.23**	.05	.04
Frank	.00	.19	-.20	-.02	.03	.25**	-.08	-.08	-.03
Careful listener	.11	.03	-.18	-.05	.07	.02	.15*	.06	.10
Informal	.01	.03	-.06	.04	.08*	.04	.08	.01	.02
Credibility									
Trustworthy	.12	-.01	-.30*	.06	.07	.08	.02	.02	.00
Informative	.07	.10	-.09	-.01	.06	.16*	-.03	.01	-.01
Dynamic	.12	.20	-.20	.00	-.04	.09	-.14*	-.04	-.05
Outcomes									
Satisfaction with focal person	.08	.11	.08	-.06	.02	.18**	.03	.02	-.03
Job satisfaction	.07			.01			-.10		
Role clarity	.08			.00			-.15*		

*p < .05.
**p < .01.

Success was also linked to peer ratings of lack of careful transmitting on the part of the focal person.

In sum, open and two-way communications with subordinates seemed to pay off in the nonprofit circumstances but not in the private sector. Superior evaluations of care in transmitting and frankness helped industrial managers, as did satisfactory relations and being regarded as informative.

9

Using the Communication Audit for Diagnosis and Remediation

As indicated in Chapter 2, the data gathered in the communication audit questionnaires completed by the focal persons and their colleagues are fed back to the focal persons. The process aims to provide diagnostic information as well as to stimulate remedial efforts by focusing attention of the focal persons on discrepancies between their self-generated data and those from their colleagues. It also calls attention to differences between actual outcomes and preferred outcomes.

Using procedures described by Bass (1960), Solomon (1976) demonstrated the positive effects of subordinates' feedback to library directors, particularly on those seemingly in most need of it. Similarly, feedback of subordinates' ratings to their superiors was employed successfully at Exxon (Maloney & Hinrichs, 1959), in a public utility (Baumgartel, 1959), and with staff employees at a university (Hegarty, 1974). Hegarty was able to employ an experimental group of supervisors who received feedback on 15 behavioral items immediately after an original survey completed by their subordinates, and a control group of supervisors who did not receive feedback. Ten weeks later, supervisors who had received feedback earned significantly higher overall ratings as supervisors from their subordinates than did the comparable control group who had not received any feedback. These results were consistent with the supervisors' belief that they had become better supervisors as a consequence of the feedback (Hegarty, 1973).

Questionnaire survey data feedback is now a common technique of the organizational development consultant, because benefits-to-costs ratios generally are highest for such survey feedback approaches to improving interpersonal relations in contrast to individual consultation or sensitivity training (e.g., Bowers, 1973; Greiner, 1972). The well-constructed questionnaire tends to provide wide coverage more economically than the interview. At the same time, it is free of dependence on the idiosyncracies of the interviewer and the interview. It seemed that feedback to focal persons of communication performance would be equally beneficial.

Propositions Concerning Use of Communication Audit

Nine propositions underlie the use of the communication audit for diagnosis and improvement.

First, on the basis of previous research, we expected that an individual focal person's communication style, credibility, and the outcomes could be described reasonably fully by the scores in the model. That is, we could have asked many more questions and generated many more scores, but most of the additional information would be redundant as far as communication and effects were concerned. We assumed our factors accounted for a large portion of the measurable variance involved in behaviorally rated interpersonal variance.

Second, we expected that our completely anonymous approach promoted the validity of the information that colleagues are willing to provide.

Third, we assumed that focal persons are not fully aware of their communication styles and effects. Self-ratings help to point up the discrepancies with reality. These discrepancies may be a central problem for focal persons. Their performances on the job are of most relevance to the organization. Special tests or peer ratings of performance in off-the-job seminars can only estimate with more or less accuracy on-the-job performance. However, performance on the test or in the seminar setting may differ systematically from that in a job setting since the focal person is playing a different role in the testing or seminar situation than on the job.

Fourth, focal persons, given suitable support, opportunity, and guidance, will be interested in taking advantage of the confirmations and disconfirmations from their colleagues about their performances in communicating. They will be more receptive to suggestions for improvement.

Fifth, individualized training and development activities can be offered, since the individual communication audits may reveal different problems for different focal persons. One focal person might do well to concentrate on improving his or her listening skills and attitudes, while another focal person concentrates on more careful transmitting.

Sixth, summary data from communication audits for pools of members in the different units of an organization make it possible to pinpoint which kinds of different communication problems need to be solved in the different units. In one unit as a whole, role clarity may be missing, hindering effectiveness; in another unit, lack of two-way communication may be the most salient difficulty. In turn, such results can guide what kinds of policies or developmental activities need to be offered.

Seventh, the opportunity to repeat a communication audit can provide a handy measure of progress to both individuals and organizations.

Eight, different communication style patterns are possible. Focal persons can be low, medium, or high on any one of the five communication style variables independently of their performances on the other four. The same is true for the three credibility scales and for the outcome measures.

Ninth, remedial action depends on what problems are revealed. For example, as noted in Chapter 4, a key to colleague role clarity is focal person credibility. This in turn depends on the quality of communications. A subsequent discussion between focal persons and their colleagues in which they each first tell the other what they think is expected of them, then see the discrepancies with what actually is expected, may have salutory effects if role clarity is low.

The Need for Feedback from Others

Chapter 3 detailed the general level of agreement among subordinates' ratings of the same focal persons. We took this as evidence of the convergent validity of subordinates' ratings. And yet, as shown in

Chapter 5, role relationships vis-à-vis the focal person also seem to shape ratings of the focal persons' communication behavior (see Table 5.4). To validate our third assumption, that we are generally unaware of how well or poorly we communicate with others, we correlated the focal persons' own ratings with those of their colleagues (subordinates, peers, and superiors) in four organizations. The first sample came from a county social service setting, but differed from the other social service personnel discussed in earlier chapters. The second sample was from the Navy civilian agency described in Chapters 3 and 4. The third sample represented the industrial firm treated in Chapters 5 and 6, and the fourth sample was the military group referred to in Chapter 7. (In certain cases, the sample sizes reported here differ somewhat from those cited earlier because of differences in analyses and the treatment of missing values.) Table 9.1 shows the correlations for these samples.

TABLE 9.1
Correlations of Focal Person's Self-Ratings with Ratings by Their Subordinates, Peers, and Superiors[a]

	Communication Audit					
	Social service personnel (focal persons = 29)			Navy civilian personnel (focal persons = 74)		
	Sub ($N = 134$)	Peer ($N = 26$)	Sup ($N = 22$)	Sub ($N = 179$)	Peer ($N = 87$)	Sup ($N = 16$)
Communication style						
Careful transmitter	−.04	.03	−.13	.10	−.25	.39
Open and two-way	−.03	−.08	.41	.21	**−.37**	.55
Frank	**.28**	.47	.25	−.05	.01	**.68**
Careful listener	**.24**	−.21	−.18	**.23**	.10	.33
Informal	−.04	−.06	.21	.02	−.08	.23
Credibility						
Trustworthy	**.38**	.38	.22	.00	.15	.25
Informative	**.57**	.18	.40	−.17	.05	.37
Dynamic	**.36**	**.75**	.48	−.01	**.42**	.41

[a]Correlations significant at the .01 level are boldface. The social service and Navy civilian samples are the same ones discussed in Chapters 3 and 4. The industrial sample was previously discussed in Chapter 7.

It can be seen that colleagues were generally less in agreement with focal persons about some communication audit variables than about others. For example, none of the 12 correlations for the extent to which the focal person was a careful transmitter or informal was significant, although it appeared as if superiors everywhere were a bit more in agreement with focal persons on these dimensions than were peers and subordinates. On the other hand, 6 of the 12 correlations about the dynamism of the focal person were significant, ranging as high as .75 between the 26 social service agency peers and their focal persons. Superiors and subordinates everywhere, except among the Naval civilian personnel, tended to agree with their focal persons about how informative the focal persons were. Frankness was another variable about which greater agreement was found between colleagues' and focal persons' ratings, while little such agreement appeared for careful

Communication Audit					
Industrial personnel (focal persons = 117)			Military officers (focal persons = 69)		
Sub ($N = 433$)	Peer ($N = 314$)	Sup ($N = 151$)	Sub ($N = 300$)	Peer ($N = 74$)	Sup ($N = 46$)
.06	.06	.19	.11	.16	.00
.00	.09	.12	−.04	.17	−.07
.10	**.22**	**.24**	.12	−.10	−.03
.18	.01	.07	.12	.05	.24
.05	.03	.14	−.04	.09	.23
.18	.13	.19	.11	.02	.06
.19	.09	**.29**	**.15**	.09	.22
.16	.08	**.30**	**.17**	.12	.23

transmitter, open and two-way, and informal. In all, while it is impossible to prove the null hypothesis, it is clear that the focal person is likely to obtain a considerably different picture of his or her communication patterns if offered by a colleague than if self-generated.

In addition to the limited agreement between self-reports and colleagues' ratings, there are strong indications that the mean level of self-reports tends to be less related to subsequent observed behavior than are superiors', peers', and subordinates' ratings (see Chapter 5). To further illustrate here the possible error arising from exclusive dependence on self-reported communication styles, we compared the scores of focal persons rating themselves and scores obtained from subordinates, peers, and superiors in the four organizations described here. For this analysis, ratings of subordinates, peers, and superiors were pooled.

Table 9.2 shows that focal persons in all four samples downgrade themselves significantly (at $p < .02$ or better) according to ANOVAs on the extent they are careful listeners. This seems to be a heretofore undiscovered finding. No ready explanation can be offered of why

TABLE 9.2
Scores on Communication Styles and Credibility as a Function of Source:
Focal Persons versus Colleagues (Analysis of Variance)[a]

	Social service personnel				Navy civilian personnel			
	Self ($N = 24$)	Colleagues ($N = 187$)	F	P	Self ($N = 74$)	Colleagues ($N = 469$)	F	P
Communication style								
Careful transmitter	6.1	6.4	1.7	.19	5.5	6.3	18.2	.00
Open and two-way	6.2	6.2	0.0	.93	6.4	6.1	2.8	.09
Frank	5.7	6.2	3.0	.09	6.0	6.5	8.2	.00
Careful listener	6.7	7.6	8.9	.00	6.8	7.4	12.3	.00
Informal	5.7	6.4	2.5	.11	6.1	6.8	9.1	.00
Credibility								
Trustworthy	7.1	7.4	1.1	.29	7.1	7.6	6.9	.01
Informative	7.2	7.7	2.0	.15	7.5	7.5	0.0	.92
Dynamic	6.3	6.9	4.3	.04	6.9	7.0	1.1	.29

[a]Responses of subordinates, peers, and superiors were pooled for this analysis. As in all data presentations, the potential range of scores is from 1 to 9.

people are more critical than their colleagues of their own tendencies to listen carefully. Perhaps we are perceived by speakers to be attending more carefully to them than we actually feel we are. Focal persons in three of the four samples also rate themselves significantly lower as careful transmitters as compared to their colleagues. Interestingly, the one dimension where focal persons consistently rate themselves as high or higher than colleagues do is for open and two-way communication, although the F value is significant in only one of the four samples.

The Feedback Process and Remedial Action

The feedback process ordinarily takes place with groups of focal persons; a workshop of say 30 focal persons in quite manageable. But, feedback can be provided as an individual counselor–client arrangement as well, or simply via a written packet of material including the data and explanatory backup to help interpret the numbers. However, this last approach of mail-back only is probably the least useful.

Industrial personnel				Military officers			
Self ($N = 113$)	Colleagues ($N = 763$)	F	P	Self ($N = 69$)	Colleagues ($N = 425$)	F	P
5.9	6.3	5.7	.02	6.2	6.7	6.7	.01
6.6	6.2	9.6	.00	6.9	6.6	1.4	.23
6.4	6.6	2.3	.13	6.4	6.8	5.6	.02
7.2	7.4	5.4	.02	7.0	7.5	12.0	.00
6.4	6.6	1.6	.21	6.9	6.9	0.0	.95
6.8	7.3	15.6	.00	7.4	7.6	1.1	.29
7.6	7.5	1.2	.28	7.7	7.8	.1	.75
7.1	7.1	0.0	.87	5.8	5.9	1.0	.30

YOUR COMMUNICATION AUDIT

FOCAL PERSON PF0063   7 COLLEAGUES   3 MISSING   NAME GEORGE JAMESON   DATE 5/09/82

COMMUNICATION STYLES — — — — — — — → CREDIBILITY — — — — — — — → OUTCOMES

FP	M	RANGE		FP	M	RANGE		FP	M	RANGE	
6	5	1–7	CAREFUL TRANSMITTER	7	5	1–8	TRUSTWORTHY	7	6	4–8	ROLE CLARITY
7	4	1–7	OPEN AND TWO-WAY	9	7	4–8	INFORMATIVE	5	5	3–6	JOB SATISFACTION
8	6	5–7	FRANK	8	7	6–8	DYNAMIC	8	5	1–8	SATISFACTION WITH FP
5	4	2–8	CAREFUL LISTENER								
8	4	2–6	INFORMAL								

KEY

9 EXTREMELY HIGH
8
7 HIGH
6
5 NEITHER HIGH NOR LOW
4
3 LOW
2
1 EXTREMELY LOW

Figure 9.1. Computer printout of results of communication audit for one focal person. (FP represents focal person; M represents mean of colleagues' ratings.) (Copyright 1975 by Transnational Program Corporation, Scottsville, New York, 14546.)

Communication Audit

The process begins with all focal persons receiving computer print-outs of their own survey results. Figure 9.1 displays a copy of such a printout.

The printout is carefully explained by the workshop leader or the counselor. On the top line is noted the number of colleagues whose questionnaires were included in the display and the number who received questionnaires but failed to return them.

Colleagues include subordinates, peers, and superiors of the focal person (which explains some of the range in responses). The pooling here is required to maintain anonymity of the colleagues responses, since usually only one superior is involved and sometimes only one peer or subordinate. Of course, special arrangements could be made to identify responses by superior, peer, and subordinate if prior agreement was obtained from the respondents and it was felt that trust level and norms for openness were sufficiently high in the organization so that identifying colleagues would not put them in jeopardy.

The next line, "Communication Styles → Credibility → Outcomes," is a summary statement of the model first presented in Chapter 2. Here we note that personal data are being provided isomorphic to the model's conceptualization. Emphasized is that satisfaction and role clarity depend on credibility and communication style. Under "FP" are the means for the focal person's own questionnaire responses for each of the dimensions extracted from the questionnaire. Thus, in Figure 9.1, George Jameson responded on those items concerning how carefully he transmits. A mean score of 6 summarized the average of his responses. This is a coded mean, rounded to the nearest digit so that all printed scores can range from 1 to 9 as in the key shown in the audit. His colleagues, on their parallel questionnaires, yield a grand mean of 5 for the items describing George Jameson as a careful transmitter. The range for his seven colleagues was from 1 to 7 on that scale.

The interpretation of scores on the audit is as follows. To eliminate decimals, and to use numbers from 1 to 9, scale scores are derived by combining scores on all items forming that scale. For scales with 7-point scaled items this was accomplished by dividing the total score obtained from adding responses across all items by the number of items forming that scale. This value was then multiplied by 1.42871 and then .75 was subtracted so that it became a number ranging from 1.00 to 9.00. This number was then rounded to a single digit on the communication audit sheet ranging from 1 to 9. Some of the outcome dimensions were derived from 5-point scaled items. For scores derived from these items, the item total for the scale was divided by the number of items in that scale. This value was then multiplied by 2, and then 1 was subtracted. The resulting value was in turn rounded to range from 1 to 9.

For all survey factors, a low score means a low amount or degree and a high score means a high amount or degree of that factor. Scores in the 4–5–6 range are best interpreted as being neither high nor low on a factor, 1–2–3 as low, and 7–8–9 as high.

Normative results such as those shown in Table 9.3 are provided to further the interpretation of results. Such a table is automatically updated and printed with each new survey completed.

Given the level of reliability indexed by the standard error of measurement, not too much meaning is attributed to score differences of a single point or even of two points in the area of the midpoint, 5. This is especially true when comparing focal persons' scores to the average scores generated by colleagues. If the focal person has a score of 4 and the colleagues have a score of 6, both are within one unit of the midpoint and it is probably best to consider them as essentially the same. On the other hand, score differences of three or greater, may be given considerable emphasis even when the midpoint is involved (e.g., a comparison of 5 and 8 or 5 and 2). It is helpful also to consider the number of colleagues and the range of their scores when large differences are noted. When the number of colleagues is small, say two or three, then one extreme score can have a large influence on the mean. This information is useful to the focal person in that it indicates that someone is "out of step" so to speak.

It can be seen from the illustration in Figure 9.1 that there was a large discrepancy between George Jameson and his colleagues on how open and two-way the manner in which he communicates with them is. He thinks he is much more open than they think he is. He also believes himself to be much more informal than they do. But in most matters, his colleagues are in wide disagreement among themselves.

Once focal persons indicate they are clear about the bases of the numbers on their own printouts, the next step is for them to extend their results to the extension form given in Appendix 9.A, pages 185–187. This makes it possible to display their own results graphically. While this display could be generated by computer, we believe that by asking focal persons to carry out this simple chore by hand, alongside

TABLE 9.3
Norms Based on 1308 Colleagues' Descriptions of Focal Persons in Industry and Government

Factor						Percentile							
						Scores							
	1	5	10	20	30	40	50	60	70	80	90	95	99
Communication style													
Careful transmitter	3[a]	4	4	5	5	6	6	6	7	7	8	8	9
Open and two-way	2	3	4	4	5	5	6	6	7	7	8	8	9
Frank	3	4	4	5	6	6	6	7	7	8	8	9	9
Careful listener	4	5	5	6	6	7	7	7	8	8	9	9	9
Informal													
Credibility													
Trustworthy	4	5	6	6	6	7	7	7	8	8	9	9	9
Informative	4	5	5	6	7	7	7	8	8	9	9	9	9
Dynamic	5	6	6	7	7	8	8	8	9	9	9	9	9
Outcomes													
Role clarity	4	5	6	6	7	7	7	7	8	8	9	9	9
Job satisfaction	2	3	4	5	6	6	7	7	7	8	9	9	9
Satisfaction with focal person	3	4	5	6	6	6	7	7	7	8	8	9	9

[a]One out of 100 focal persons were described by their colleagues with a mean value of 3 in careful transmitting; 99% of focal persons were described as above 3 on the average.

behavioral definitions of each dimension of the model, we ensure that focal persons give all their own data some attention.

Reflecting on Feedback

We then ask focal persons to consider several questions, first by themselves, then, if in a workshop feedback situation, to share their conclusions in peer groups with two or three peers. In workshops, this arrangement permits the opportunity to obtain peer guidance and reflected opinions.

Two or three questions of the nine below are considered alone, then in groups, before going on to a second set of two or three.

1. Which audit results do you feel best about?
2. Which outcomes are most bothersome to you?
3. Where are the biggest discrepancies between you and your colleagues? Among your colleagues as shown by the range of their scores?
4. How satisfied are you with your communication style patterns as seen by you and as seen by your colleagues?
5. What would an ideal audit look like for a focal person in your position? How does yours differ from the ideal audit?
6. Can you perceive a message coming through from your colleagues? In other words, are they trying to tell you something?
7. If you could change some scores by changing yourself, which ones would you want to change?
8. What action steps do you think you can take to bring about the desired changes?
9. Based on your analysis of your audit, what are you going to say to your colleagues?

The questions are designed to help a focal person concentrate on major problem areas and issues of potential concern. Besides exposing potential problem areas, the audit provides ideas for improvement by suggesting what focal persons might do immediately to correct some of their communication difficulties. The staff may then suggest additional remedial action as well as available short courses, tapes, films, or readings on effective communicating.

Remedial Action[1]

Specifically, here are examples of what may be suggested to focal persons who have been given diagnostic feedback from their colleagues that one or more of their communication styles or credibility are relatively low in comparison to their peers on workshop, organizational, or national norms.

CAREFUL TRANSMITTING

One way to improve one's performance as a careful transmitter is to avoid telling people they *always* have to be reminded to attend the weekly staff meeting or they *never* seem to get things right. What "things"? And "never"? That is, focal persons should try to avoid talking in very general terms. On the contrary, they should try to cite specific examples to illustrate their points. A soft, nonthreatening tone will be more effective. Avoiding talking too fast will help as well. In talking to people for whom English is a second language, it is important to speak more slowly, not more loudly, to avoid slang, and to enunciate more definitively. Outlining in advance what one wants to say, asking for questions, and using other rhetorical procedures also are likely to increase one's effectiveness in transmitting information.

OPEN AND TWO-WAY

Focal persons can improve their performances in several ways on this dimension. First, they need to make more use of open questions allowing for a wide range of answers. They need to seek opinion and allow colleagues to restate or summarize the understanding of what the focal person has tried to communicate to them. Instead of telling colleagues what to do and how to do it, it is often more useful to ask colleagues how they view the problem, how they plan to cope with it, and how the focal person can help.

Two-way exchange is promoted by focal persons who keep colleagues from feeling threatened. We are more comfortable with those with whom we are more familiar. As seen in Chapter 5, familiarity due to frequency of contact promotes the tendency to communicate openly

[1]Ideas for this section have been taken from a variety of sources, but particularly helpful has been Buening, 1974.

and in two-way exchange. In addition to experiencing unfamiliarity as a threat, colleagues will feel threatened if they see themselves interrupted, criticized, evaluated, or argued with every time they attempt to continue to converse with the focal person.

FRANK

Often people are unwilling to say what they feel for fear of retaliation or unpleasant reaction. Focal persons who want to be more frank need to take chances to see that the effects are not as bad as they anticipated. Colleagues usually prefer openness to hiding behind polite facades. Naturally, brutal frankness can be punishing and punished in return. In such instances focal persons need to understand that, while such a level of frankness may satisfy their own egos, it is likely to be destructive in the longer run.

CAREFUL LISTENING

Listening should be active. Focal persons can demonstrate care in listening by restating to colleagues in their own words what they understood the colleagues to be saying. This check for meaning demonstrates interest and helps colleagues to explain their positions more fully. Focal persons can show colleagues they have heard, understood, and remembered what was said by summarizing the exchange.

Careful listening also involves attention to nonverbal clues. Such obvious ones as yawning from seeming boredom should be questioned for meaning. More ambiguous ones, such as loss of eye contact, should be observed without comment. Throughout, focal persons need to be sensitive to feelings. Often opening up discussion about such feelings results in more rational discussion subsequent to the ventilation of emotions.

According to Nichols and Stevens (1957), the careful listener tries to anticipate what the conversation is leading to and what conclusions are likely to be drawn; the listener weighs the evidence used by the speaker to support the speaker's points. At intervals, the listener reviews and mentally summarizes what has been said so far; the listener searches for meaning that may not be in the spoken words.

One should listen for ideas as well as facts. Messages need to be understood in their contexts. And most important, careful listeners guard against what they know to be their own personal filters and biases, such as hearing what they want to hear rather than what they should hear (Duker, 1970; Keefe, 1971).

INFORMAL

Transactional analysis points to the utility of treating other adults as peers, neither as children nor parents. Focal persons should consider how they would like colleagues to talk to them and attempt to pursue a similar level of informality. If focal persons want to be addressed by first name, they should address colleagues in the same way.

Merely being told what can be done to improve one's communication skills obviously is unlikely to produce much improvement. The desire to improve must be there. We think that this desire is heightened by the diagnostic feedback. But again, more must be done. Skills require practice. Practice requires taking chances that mistakes made will be tolerable. Skill learning requires subsequent feedback. Some of this no doubt occurs when colleagues are seen by focal persons to respond differently than before, as focal persons attempt to change their styles, but focal persons must be alert to such differences in response from their colleagues. A rediagnosis in 3–6 months can also be helpful in providing evidence of the extent focal persons may have changed.

Summary

The communication audit provides the basis for a questionnaire survey feedback to focal persons, individually or in workshops. The process is likely both to identify areas of need as well as to sensitize persons to them. Further, it generates interest in taking various kinds of actions toward self-improvement suggested by the diagnostic data.

Appendix 9.A: Communication Audit—Extension Form

This form is for your own use to provide a different display of your scores to help in your interpretation of their meaning.

Place a square around the score representing your self-ratings which you registered according to your computer print-out profile. Circle the score representing your colleagues' mean. Note their range with brackets. Norms for a group of focal persons to be provided by staff persons can be shown by arrow.

The example below shows that you have a score of 3. Your colleagues' mean is 4. Their range is 2 to 7. The group norm was 6.

$$1 : (2 : \boxed{3} : \text{④} : 5 : \underset{\uparrow}{6} : 7) : 8 : 9$$

Focal Person's Communication Style

	Score
CAREFUL TRANSMITTER—careful in organizing one's thoughts and choosing appropriate words when commmunicating with others	1 : 2 : 3 : 4 : 5 : 6 : 7 : 8 : 9 _____
OPEN, TWO-WAY COMMUNICA-TOR—encouraging, using a style of open, free flow of two-way communi-cations.	1 : 2 : 3 : 4 : 5 : 6 : 7 : 8 : 9 _____
FRANK—frank levelling with others, self-assured in one's communication with others.	1 : 2 : 3 : 4 : 5 : 6 : 7 : 8 : 9 _____
CAREFUL LISTENER—attentive in listening to others.	1 : 2 : 3 : 4 : 5 : 6 : 7 : 8 : 9 _____
INFORMAL—natural, relaxed, informal style of communicating.	1 : 2 : 3 : 4 : 5 : 6 : 7 : 8 : 9 _____

Focal Person's Credibility

	Score
TRUSTWORTHY—congenial, fair, kind and just in dealings with others.	1 : 2 : 3 : 4 : 5 : 6 : 7 : 8 : 9 _____
INFORMATIVE—knowledgeable, experienced, authoritative and skilled in communicating with others.	1 : 2 : 3 : 4 : 5 : 6 : 7 : 8 : 9 _____
DYNAMIC—forceful, active, energetic and not hesitant or timid in commu-nicating with others.	1 : 2 : 3 : 4 : 5 : 6 : 7 : 8 : 9 _____

	Score
ROLE CLARITY—colleagues know what they are expected to do on their job and colleagues know what to expect if they do their job as ex-pected.	1 : 2 : 3 : 4 : 5 : 6 : 7 : 8 : 9 _____

JOB SATISFACTION—overall satisfaction of the focal person and overall satisfaction of his colleagues with their respective assignments.	1 : 2 : 3 : 4 : 5 : 6 : 7 : 8 : 9 _____
SATISFACTION WITH EACH OTHER—satisfaction of the focal person with his colleagues, and satisfaction of his colleagues with the focal person.	1 : 2 : 3 : 4 : 5 : 6 : 7 : 8 : 9 _____

10

Conclusion

Additional Questions

In this program of investigation, we proceeded from interviews and questionnaires about managerial communication to a refined questionnaire schedule to tap communication style, credibility, and outcomes. Certain methodological questions arose during the course of this research, several of which were dealt with in Chapters 2 and 3. Additional questions concerning response bias, sampling bias, and leniency effects should also be noted, since they can influence our conclusions. These issues are briefly discussed below.

Response Bias

Individual raters may differ in the extent they use such extremes as always and never, or lower rather than higher values, so that a positive correlation emerges among the dimensions due to the rater. Our approach of having several colleagues of a focal person complete the questionnaires and then using mean scores for analysis reduces this potential difficulty, since a range of response tendencies is likely to be included in a typical group of colleague respondents. The extent to which this is a problem cannot be determined, but we note that the issue is one that faces all organizational research based on perceptual data.

Sampling Bias

To combine data gathering with data feedback, as we described in Chapter 2, focal persons were asked to hand out questionnaires to be completed about themselves to all colleagues (up to 10) who knew them well enough to rate them. Using this procedure rather than random or accidental sampling yielded response rates often as high as 80%, a figure in marked contrast to many industrial surveys that must depend on 20% response rates. In order to determine whether any bias is introduced by our standard data gathering procedure, an alternative strategy might be employed where focal persons would be asked to identify *all* their colleagues (*colleagues* being defined as persons one interacts with as part of the job at least once a week). Then the researcher could ask the focal persons to identify colleagues they had planned to have rate them using our standard instructions for such requests (i.e., know you well enough to rate you). *All* colleagues could then be given the questionnaires, and analyses could be made that compared responses about focal persons from colleagues selected by the focal persons and from the remainder of colleagues. While it is impossible to prove the hypothesis of no difference, this alternative process could help to establish the lack of practical implication of the difference.

Our present view on the seriousness of this issue is that, as shown in Chapter 5, whether colleague raters are subordinates, peers, or superiors is likely to make much more of a difference than is the method for handing out questionnaires. Hence, while this potential sampling problem is recognized, it may not be particularly severe.

Leniency

Another potential bias in the data collection process is that, instead of rating the quality of communication behavior, colleagues may be merely reflecting overall lenient or severe judgments of particular focal persons. This is an issue that confronts most research of this type. One

TABLE 10.1
Validated Leniency Items[a, b]

---

1. He's always willing to admit it when he makes a mistake.[c]
2. He always tries to practice what he preaches.
3. He doesn't seem to find it difficult to get along with loud mouthed, obnoxious people.
4. He sometimes tries to get even, rather than forgive and forget. (R)[d]
5. When he doesn't know something, he doesn't mind at all admitting it.
6. He is always courteous, even to people who are disagreeable.
7. At times he has really insisted on having things his own way. (R)
8. He would never think of letting someone else be blamed for his mistakes.
9. He never hesitates to go out of his way to help people in trouble.
10. He has never shown intense dislike for anyone.
11. He sometimes seems resentful when he doesn't get his way. (R)
12. He is always careful about his manner of dress.
13. His social manners are always perfect.
14. If he could get something without paying for it and be sure that he was not seen, he would probably do it. (R)
15. He likes to gossip at times. (R)
16. No matter who he's talking to, he's always a good listener.
17. There have been occasions when he took advantage of someone. (R)
18. He never resents being asked to return a favor.
19. He never gets irked when people express ideas very different from his.
20. There are times when he seems to get quite jealous of the good fortune of others. (R)
21. He almost never tells someone off.
22. He sometimes gets irritated by people who ask favors of him. (R)
23. He has never deliberately said something that hurt someone's feelings.

---

[a]From C. A. Schreisheim, A. J. Kinicki, and J. F. Schreisheim, The effect of leniency on leader behavior descriptions, *Organizational Behavior and Human Performance*, 1979, *23*, p. 13.

[b]The instructions used with this scale are as follows:

Listed below are a number of statements concerning personal attitudes and traits. Read each item and decide whether it is true or false as it pertains to your immediate supervisor or superior. If you do not have firsthand knowledge of some of these attitudes and traits, use your overall impression of your supervisor to decide whether it is true or false. Check each item in the true *or* false column, but *not* both. Do *not* omit or skip any items.

[c]Responses scored True = 1 and False = 0.

[d]The symbol (R) designates a reflected (reverse-scored) item.

approach for dealing with the problem has been through the use of a leniency scale (Schriescheim, Kinicki, & Schriesheim, 1979). Table 10.1 lists the items in this scale. Higher agreement expressed on each item indicates a greater degree of leniency.

We included this scale in one of our surveys of social service personnel. Responses from 32 subordinates describing their superiors were included in the analysis. Leniency correlated as follows with the measures in the communication model:

Correlation with leniency	Communication model variables
Communication style	
.27	careful transmitter
.56	open and two-way
.35	frank
.56	careful listener
.38	informal
Credibility	
.70	trustworthy
.34	informative
.09	dynamic
Outcomes	
.19	role clarity
.67	satisfaction with focal person
.38	job satisfaction

It should be noted that a few of the items in the leniency scale developed by Schriescheim *et al.* have considerable communication style overtones (e.g., Items 16 and 19). Hence, the moderately high correlations are not surprising. Some of the credibility and outcome scales, such as trustworthiness and satisfaction with focal person, were also strongly correlated with leniency, although once again an examination of some of the items indicates considerable overlap with selected items in our own instrument. Some of the other scales, on the other hand, such as dynamic and role clarity, were largely independent of the leniency measure.

A central question was to what extent leniency itself accounted for the interrelations among the scales. Thus, for example, if trustworthiness and satisfaction with the focal persons both correlated highly with leniency, was there any communality left between trustworthiness and satisfaction if leniency was partialled out of the relation? Table 10.2 shows the results of correlations among pairs of the communication model variables after leniency has been partialled out of one of the variables. It can be seen that some relations were considerably modified, while others were relatively unchanged as a consequence of the partialling. Thus, the relations of dynamic with other variables were unchanged, while correlations with trustworthiness dropped in half, though they still remained sizable.

If these sample results are indicative of the effect, then it may be useful to explore further the development of a leniency type scale to adjust for the leniency effects.

In sum, these additional potential bias issues are recognized here as having possible implications for our findings. Our judgment on this matter is that some support can be found for these alternative explanations, but not enough to greatly reduce confidence in the conclusions we have presented in earlier chapters.

Conclusion

Throughout this book, we have noted that the process of communication is dynamic and complex. Moreover, since communication permeates just about everything we do in organizations, it is difficult to isolate it from the larger context within which it occurs. Hence, we find in the literature multiple perspectives, approaches, and terminology applied to similar or overlapping activities.

We have discussed this issue in considerable detail in a review of the literature in Chapter 1, where we attempted to bring together a portion of the communication literature that focuses particularly on interpersonal communication behavior. The development of the communication model portrayed in Chapter 2 thus represents an effort to synthesize various concerns and research findings in a way that focuses attention on the outcomes of interpersonal communication behavior in organizational settings.

Of particular concern to us in this effort has been the attempt to operationalize concepts that have been used in the communication literature into specific behaviorally oriented descriptive statements that can be used to characterize a person's communication style. Thus, perhaps most important in this entire research endeavor has been our concern with getting a concrete set of measures that characterize interpersonal communication behavior. The five dimensions of communication style identified and developed in Chapters 2 and 3 appear to capture fairly well key aspects of verbal communication interaction. Moreover, the general validity and reliability of these measures across organizational settings (as noted in Chapter 3) suggests that these measures can be usefully applied in a variety of organizational contexts. In addition, the application in Chapter 4 of these measures of com-

TABLE 10.2
First-Order and Partial Correlations among the Communication Audit Variables
Subtracting the Effect of Leniency (N = 32 Subordinates)

	First-Order and Partial Product Moment Correlations[a, b]				
	Careful transmitter	Open and two-way	Frank	Careful listener	Informal
Careful transmitter		.33	.16	.27	.21
Open and two-way	.23		**.57**	**.58**	**.68**
Frank	.08	.48		**.45**	**.55**
Careful listener	.18	**.45**	.35		**.62**
Informal	.12	**.60**	**.48**	**.55**	
Trustworthy	−.04	**.47**	−.05	.27	**.42**
Informative	.14	.31	**.43**	.11	.36
Dynamic	.18	.16	**.47**	−.21	.11
Role clarity	.04	.38	.27	.04	.09
Job satisfaction	.08	**.58**	**.46**	.28	**.43**
Satisfaction with focal person	.00	**.54**	**.48**	.29	.38

[a]Zero-order correlations are reported in the upper right hand triangle. Partial correlations are reported in the lower triangle.

[b]Correlations are boldface when $p < .01$.

munication style and the model as a whole suggests that they fairly well predict the types of outcomes proposed in the model.

The strength of the causal argument presented in the model has been only partially explored, although tentative support is indicated in Chapter 4. However, in a broader sense, we recognize, as with so many other facets of organizational life, the reciprocal nature of the interpersonal communication process. Thus, while interpersonal communication style may help to shape the credibility of the communicator and impact role clarity and satisfaction, such impact in turn can feed back to influence communication style, as well as perceptions thereof. Nevertheless, the model does offer concrete direction in terms of how one might interrupt this reciprocal process by modifying one's communication style, which in turn can subsequently affect credibility and consequences.

First-Order and Partial Product Moment Correlations [a, b]

Trustworthy	Informative	Dynamic	Role clarity	Job satisfaction	Satisfaction with focal person
.14	.22	.17	.09	.23	.11
.66	.47	.29	.42	.73	.64
.18	.51	.44	.31	.55	.56
.46	.27	−.20	.11	.48	.42
.54	.46	.10	.16	.55	.48
	.29	.03	.27	.61	.47
.03		.50	.31	.71	.32
.04	.55		.55	.43	.24
.21	.49	.56		.49	.06
.31	.64	.58	.50		.68
.28	.20	.27	−.03	.59	

This is not to ignore other elements, such as technology, work group size, and other interpersonal factors than can influence the process. As noted in the later chapters of this book, such factors can be shown to have certain kinds of influence. However, sufficient research has not yet been done to allow for prescriptive guidance in dealing with all these contextual factors.

The research reported here takes some initial steps in this direction. At the same time, the feedback that can be provided to the participating focal person as data is collected via the survey instrument helps to promote greater attention by practicing managers to a vital aspect of their work. Hence, this research strategy has a practical, immediate focus as well as a broader theory-building concern. In combination, the approach appears to hold promise for both practitioners as well as researchers.

Focal Person Questionnaire

This questionnaire was the core instrument used for collecting data from focal persons. Supplemental sections were added in certain organizations. Such sections are included at the conclusion of the chapters where the data are reported.

FOCAL PERSON'S COMMUNICATIONS SURVEY

F P   1954

Rudi Klauss
Bernard M. Bass

You have received a number of survey questionnaires to be completed by you and your colleagues. From these, your own Communications Audit will be constructed and returned to you. To ensure the accuracy of the audit the following instructions must be carefully followed:

1. The survey with a *Black* stripe is *yours* and should be completed by you and returned in the addressed envelope provided.

2. The surveys without a stripe are to be distributed to colleagues in the following priority:
   a. If you have 9 or more subordinates, distribute 1 survey to your immediate supervisor and the remaining 9 surveys to subordinates whom you feel know you best.
   b. If you have less than 9 subordinates, distribute 1 survey to your immediate supervisor, 1 to each of your subordinates, and the remaining surveys to other colleagues whom you feel know you best.
   c. If you have no subordinates, distribute 1 survey to your immediate supervisor, and up to 9 surveys (minimum of 3) to colleagues whom you feel know you best.

   The completed surveys are to be returned directly by your colleagues in the addressed envelopes provided.

3. Before distributing the survey questionnaires to your colleagues you must *first* record the serial number that is in the upper left corner of their cover page in the spaces provided below. If, for example, you have five colleagues to whom you gave surveys, then their five serial numbers should appear in the spaces provided below. This information will permit the calculation of your profile to provide direct feedback to you.

   The purpose of the survey is to obtain a review of how you communicate in the work situation. There are questions about how you communicate to your colleagues and what effects your communications have on them. Your colleagues will answer similar questions.

   On your audit your views will be compared with those of your colleagues taken as a group. THE RESPONSES OF YOUR INDIVIDUAL COLLEAGUES WILL BE COMPLETELY ANONYMOUS.

YOUR NAME (PLEASE PRINT)		YOUR BUSINESS MAILING ADDRESS	
	FIRST _____		_____
	M.I. _____		_____
	LAST _____		_____

*You can use a fictitious name or none at all as long as you make note of your own code number.

IMPORTANT

In the spaces below write the serial numbers of the *unstriped* questionnaires you have *before* distributing them to your colleagues. If possible, allow your colleagues to select their questionnaires so you have no way of identifying their individual code numbers.

_____   _____

_____   _____

_____   _____

_____   _____

_____   _____

PART A: BIOGRAPHICAL INFORMATION

To the left of each item is a blank. Select the most appropriate response and write its number in the blank.

Example: ___1___ Sex: 1. Male

2. Female (The "1" in the blank indicates the respondent is a male.)

_____ 1. Sex: 1. Male   2. Female

_____ 2. Education: 1. Less than 8   5. 11   9. 3 years college   12. Master's Degree
            (number of years) 2. 8   6. 12   10. 4 years college   13. Beyond Master's
                               3. 9   7. 1 year college 11. more than 4 but   but no Ph.D.
                               4. 10   8. 2 years college   no advanced degree   14. Ph.D.

_____ 3. What is the primary function of your department/division/unit?

    1. Production   6. Client service
    2. Purchasing   7. General administration
    3. Research & development   8. Finance/accounting
    4. Sales, marketing, advertising, public relations   9. Personnel/training
    5. Engineering design   10. Other (please specify) _____

_____ 4. Approximately how many people work in the department/division/unit described in item #3?

_____ 5. Age:

_____ 6. Years of full time employment.

_____ 7. Years of service in present company or agency.

_____ 8. Current Annual Salary*

_____ 9. How long (in months) have you been at this salary level?

_____ 10. Starting salary in present company or agency*

_____ 11. Approximately how many levels are below you in this organization (your organization is the name that is on your letterhead)?

_____ 12. How many members, including the boss, are there in your work group (the group in which you and others at your level report to a common superior)?

_____ 13. How many people report directly to you (i.e., on the level directly below to you)?

     14. During the past four years, how many changes in position within the organization have you had:
_____   promotions to a higher level?
_____   lateral transfers (at the same level)?
_____   demotions (to a lower level)?

*Optional. Leave blank if you do not wish to answer.

PART ICS

The items in this section describe behaviors which people may exhibit when they communicate with colleagues in an organizational setting. You are asked to *respond to these items as they apply to your own behavior.* In the blank space next to each statement write the number which best describes *how frequently* you behave or act that way.

The numbers represent the following descriptive terms:

$$7 = \text{Always}$$
$$6 = \text{Constantly}$$
$$5 = \text{Usually}$$
$$4 = \text{Fairly often}$$
$$3 = \text{Sometimes}$$
$$2 = \text{Once in a while}$$
$$1 = \text{Never}$$
$$0 = \text{Cannot say, don't know}$$

Example:

___6___   I encourage others to speak their mind.
(The "6" indicates that I *constantly* encourage others to speak their mind.)

_____   1. I interrupt with my own comments before others can finish a statement.

_____   2. I speak deliberately when I communicate.

_____   3. I dominate discussions.

_____   4. I choose my words carefully.

_____   5. I ask for others' views on problems and issues.

_____   6. I keep my mind on what the speaker is saying.

_____   7. I am very informal and relaxed when I communicate.

_____   8. I organize my thoughts before I speak.

_____   9. I am frank in saying what I really think.

_____   10. My comments are brief and to the point.

_____   11. I am polished in my choice of words.

_____   12. I go out of my way to find out information which may be relevant to my work responsibilities.

_____   13. I follow up conversations with feedback.

_____   14. I jump to conclusions before all the information is presented.

_____   15. I am very natural in the way I relate to others.

_____   16. I give others feedback on their suggestions and comments.

_____   17. I tend to run off at the mouth.

_____   18. I say what I think without mincing words.

_____   19. I am receptive to points of view which differ from mine.

_____   20. I take a lot of words to say something which could be said in a very few words.

_____   21. I convey self-confidence in expressing my views.

_____   22. I let others finish their point before I comment.

_____   23. I level with others when I disagree with their viewpoints.

_____   24. I fidget when people speak to me.

_____   25. I drift from topic to topic during the course of a conversation.

PART GS

The statements in this part pertain to your subordinates' or colleagues' work situation and your general pattern of interaction with them. Some are mainly about your subordinates' or colleagues' job responsibilities, while others concern your own views about your behavior and actions towards your subordinates' or colleagues. In the blank space next to each statement write the number which best describes the extent to which you agree or disagree with that particular statement.

The numbers represent the following:

7 = Completely agree
6 = Very much agree
5 = Moderately agree
4 = Neither agree nor disagree; undecided
3 = Moderately disagree
2 = Very much disagree
1 = Completely disagree

_____ 1. I tend to be a very congenial person.

_____ 2. I think I am very well trained for my job.

_____ 3. My subordinates* know what their job responsibilities are.

_____ 4. I am very aggressive in my work.

_____ 5. I am very well qualified for my job.

_____ 6. I am a very agreeable person.

_____ 7. My subordinates* feel certain about how much authority they have.

_____ 8. I am a very hesitant person.

_____ 9. I consider myself to be very friendly.

_____ 10. I am very well informed on issues concerning my areas of responsibility.

_____ 11. Explanations are clear to my subordinates concerning their areas of responsibility.

_____ 12. I am very energetic in my job.

_____ 13. I tend to be very pleasant company.

_____ 14. I think I have the appropriate prior experience necessary for my job.

_____ 15. I am a timid person.

_____ 16. I feel that I am very fair in my dealings on the job.

_____ 17. My subordinates* know exactly what is expected of them in their job.

_____ 18. My subordinates* know that they have divided their time properly.

_____ 19. I am a very gentle person with my subordinates.*

_____ 20. I am very authoritative concerning issues which arise at work.

_____ 21. I am very just in my dealings on the job.

_____ 22. I am a very forceful person.

_____ 23. I am very skilled in my work.

_____ 24. I am very active at work.

_____ 25. I am very kind with my subordinates.*

_____ 26. My subordinates* have clear, planned goals and objectives for their jobs.

*If you have no subordinates, respond to this statement as it applies to your colleagues.

PART EF

The statements in this part are about effectiveness and satisfaction. You will be asked to judge how effective various aspects of your work situation are, or how satisfied you are with them. In the blank space next to each statement write the number which best describes your overall judgment about the statement.

_____ 1. The overall work effectiveness of your unit can be classified as:

_____ 2. Compared to all other units you have ever known, how do you rate the effectiveness of your unit?

_____ 3. How effective do you think you are in meeting the job-related needs of the people who work with you?

_____ 4. How effective do you think you are in meeting the requirements of the organization?

Use the scale below for items 1-4:

5 = Extremely Effective
4 = Very Effective
3 = Effective
2 = Only Slightly Effective
1 = Not Effective

_____ 5. All in all, how satisfied are you with this organization compared to others you know?

_____ 6. All in all, how satisfied are you with your job?

_____ 7. How satisfied do you feel with your chances for getting ahead in this organization _in the future?_

_____ 8. How satisfied are you that your own interests and abilities are being effectively used by the job you have?

_____ 9. How satisfied do you feel with the progress you have made in the organization up to now?

_____ 10. All in all, how satisfied are you with your colleagues?

_____ 11. In general, how satisfied are you that the methods of relating to others that you use are the right ones for getting work done?

Use the scale below for items 5-11:

5 = Very Satisfied
4 = Fairly Satisfied
3 = Neither Satisfied nor Dissatisfied
2 = Somewhat Dissatisfied
1 = Very Dissatisfied

_____ 12. To make your work unit the most effective unit you have ever known, to what degree are improvements needed?

Use the scale below for item 12:

5 = Very High Degree
4 = High Degree
3 = Moderate Degree
2 = Slight Degree
1 = Very Low Degree

Colleague Questionnaire

This questionnaire was the core instrument used for collecting data from colleagues (subordinates, peers, and superiors) of focal persons. Supplemental sections were added in certain organizations. These additional sections are included at the conclusion of the chapters where the data are reported.

C **9353**   *Do not sign your name anywhere on this questionnaire*

COLLEAGUES' COMMUNICATION SURVEY Rudi Klauss
Bernard M. Bass

This survey questionnaire will be used to construct an audit of the communication style that will be of help to the person you are describing. It may also be used to provide you with a capsule summary of the general level of communication effectiveness in your situation. You are requested to complete it anonymously.

The person you are describing beginning on the next page is *your focal person*, the person on whom this questionnaire is to be focused. You are asked about his or her style of communicating and what you generally think about him or her. You are also asked about your own situation.

Your focal person will answer the same questions and be able to compare how much he or she sees things the same or differently than his or her colleagues. But no individual answers will be provided. Only group results for all colleagues combined will be calculated and printed.

When you have completed the questionnaire return it as provided.

PART A: Your background and work situation

To the left of each item is a blank. Select the most appropriate response and write its number in the blank.

Example: ___1___ Sex: 1. Male   2. Female (The "1" in the blank indicates the respondent is a male)

_____ 1. Sex   1. Male   2. Female

_____ 2. Education: 1. Less than 8   5. 11   9. 3 years college   12. Master's Degree
         (number of years)   2. 8   6. 12   10. 4 years college   13. Beyond Master's
                             3. 9   7. 1 year college 11. more than 4 but   but no Ph.D.
                             4. 10   8. 2 years college   no advanced degree 14. Ph.D

_____ 3. What is the primary function of your department/division/unit?
         1. Production   6. Client service
         2. Purchasing   7. General administration
         3. Research & development   8. Finance/accounting
         4. Logistics   9. Personnel/training
         5. Engineering   10. Other (please specify) _____

_____ 4. What is your organizational relationship with your focal person? He or she is:
         1. My immediate superior   4. Higher-up (in a level above my superior's)
         2. At the same level as I am   5. Lower down (in a level below my immediate subordinates)
         3. My immediate subordinate   6. Not a member of my organization

_____ 5. How well do you know the focal person?
         1. A little   2. Some   3. Considerably   4. Very much   5. Completely

_____ 6. How close is your desk or work space to that of the focal person?
         1. Close   2. Near by
            (within 100 feet)   (over 100 feet, but same floor)
         3. Different floor,   4. Separate building
            same building

_____ 7. How long have you been associated with the focal person?
         1. Under 6 mo.   2. 6 mo. to yr.   3. 1-2 yrs.   4. over 2 years

_____ 8. How often do you interact with the focal person during a typical week?
         1. Once in awhile   2. Sometimes   3. Fairly many times
         4. Very frequently   5. Continually

_____ 9. Your Age

         10. Of the total communications   _____ % 1. Written
             you receive from the focal person   _____ % 2. Face-to-face alone
             approximately what percentage is: _____ % 3. in a group
                                                   _____ % 4. Telephone
                                                   100 %

         11. Of the total communications   _____ % 1. immediate job/
             you receive from the focal person   task related
             approximately what percentage is: _____ % 2. other organizational
                                                   _____ % 3. personal/social
                                                   100 %

PART ICS

The items in this section describe behaviors which people may exhibit when they communicate with others in an organizational setting. You are asked to *respond to these items as they apply to your focal person.* In the blank space next to each statement write the number which best describes *how frequently* your focal person behaves or acts that way.

The numbers represent the following descriptive terms:

> 7 = Always
> 6 = Constantly
> 5 = Usually
> 4 = Fairly often
> 3 = Sometimes
> 2 = Once in a while
> 1 = Never
> 0 = Cannot say, don't know

Example:

____6____ He (she)* encourages others to speak their mind.
(The respondent's "6" indicates that the focal person *constantly* encourages others to speak their mind.)

____ 1. He interrupts with his own comments before others can finish a statement.

____ 2. He speaks deliberately when he communicates.

____ 3. He dominates discussions.

____ 4. He chooses his words carefully.

____ 5. He asks for my own views on problems and issues.

____ 6. He keeps his mind on what the speaker is saying.

____ 7 He is very informal and relaxed when he communicates.

____ 8. He organizes his thoughts before he speaks.

____ 9. He is frank in saying what he really thinks.

____ 10. His comments are brief and to the point.

____ 11. He is polished in his choice of words.

____ 12. He goes out of his way to find out information which may be relevant to his work responsibilities.

____ 13. He follows up conversations with feedback.

____ 14. He jumps to conclusions before all the information is presented.

____ 15. He is very natural in the way he relates to others.

____ 16. He gives me feedback on my suggestions and comments.

____ 17. He tends to run off at the mouth.

____ 18. He says what he thinks without mincing words.

____ 19. He is receptive to points of view which differ from his.

____ 20. He takes a lot of words to say something which could be said in a very few words.

____ 21. He conveys self-confidence in expressing his views.

____ 22. He lets me finish my point before he comments.

____ 23. He levels with others when he disagrees with their viewpoints.

____ 24. He fidgets when people speak to him.

____ 25. He drifts from topic to topic during the course of a conversation.

*It should be understood that the focal person can be a man or a woman. For convenience, the person will be referred to as "he".

PART GS

The statements in this part pertain to your work and your focal person. Some are mainly about your own job responsibilities, while others concern your own views about your focal person's actions at work. In the blank space next to each statement write the number which best describes the extent to which you agree or disagree with that particular statement.

The numbers represent the following:

7 = Completely agree
6 = Very much agree
5 = Moderately agree
4 = Neither agree nor disagree; undecided
3 = Moderately disagree
2 = Very much disagree
1 = Completely disagree

_____ 1. He tends to be a very congenial person.

_____ 2. I think he is very well trained for his (her) job.

_____ 3. I know what my own job responsibilities are.

_____ 4. He is very aggressive in his work.

_____ 5. He is very well qualified for his job.

_____ 6. He is a very agreeable person.

_____ 7. I feel certain about how much authority I have.

_____ 8. He is a very hesitant person.

_____ 9. I consider him to be very friendly.

_____ 10. He is very well informed on issues concerning his areas of responsibility.

_____ 11. Explanations are clear to me concerning what I have to do.

_____ 12. He is very energetic in his job.

_____ 13. He tends to be very pleasant company.

_____ 14. I think he has the appropriate prior experience necessary for his job.

_____ 15. He is a timid person at work.

_____ 16. I think he is very fair in his dealings on the job.

_____ 17. I know exactly what is expected of me in my job.

_____ 18. I know that I have divided my time properly.

_____ 19. He is very gentle with me.

_____ 20. He is very authoritative concerning issues which arise at work.

_____ 21. He is very just in his dealings on the job.

_____ 22. He is a very forceful person.

_____ 23. He is very skilled in his work.

_____ 24. He is very active at work.

_____ 25. He is very kind to me.

_____ 26. I have clear, planned goals and objectives for my job.

PART ES

The statements in this part are about effectiveness and satisfaction. You will be asked to judge how effective various aspects of your work situation are, or how satisfied you are with them. In the blank space next to each statement write the number which best describes your overall judgment about the statement.

_____ 1. The overall effectiveness of your relations with your focal person can be classified as:

_____ 2. Compared to all other communicators you have ever known, how do you rate the effectiveness of your focal person?

_____ 3. How effective is your focal person in meeting the job-related needs of the people who interact with him (her)?

_____ 4. How effective is your focal person in meeting the requirements of the organization?

Use the scale below for items 1-4:

5 = Extremely Effective
4 = Very Effective
3 = Effective
2 = Only Slightly Effective
1 = Not Effective

_____ 5. All in all, how satisfied are you with this organization compared to others you know?

_____ 6. All in all, how satisfied are you with your job?

_____ 7. How satisfied do you feel with your chances for getting ahead in this organization _in the future?_

_____ 8. How satisfied are you that your own interests and abilities are being effectively used by the job you have?

_____ 9. How satisfied do you feel with the progress you have made in the organization up to now?

_____ 10. All in all, how satisfied are you with your focal person?

_____ 11. In general, how satisfied are you that the way the focal person interacts with you is the right way for getting your job done?

Use the scale below for items 5-11:

5 = Very Satisfied
4 = Fairly Satisfied
3 = Neither Satisfied nor Dissatisfied
2 = Somewhat Dissatisfied
1 = Very Dissatisfied

_____ 12. To make your work unit the most effective unit you have ever known, to what degree are improvements needed?

Use the scale below for item 12:

5 = Very High Degree
4 = High Degree
3 = Moderate Degree
2 = Slight Degree
1 = Very Low Degree

Means and Standard Deviations for Selected Organizations[1]

The attached norms for several selected organizations provide means and standard deviations on the measures included in the communication model. These samples come from a range of organizations with different types of missions and personnel. The first organization is the Navy civilian agency discussed in Chapters 3, 4, and 5. The second and third samples are those referred to in Chapter 6. The fourth sample represents personnel from one of the two military bases discussed in Chapter 7, while the fifth sample comes from a social service agency setting that has not been treated elsewhere.

Three sets of means and standard deviations are provided for each organization: for all colleagues combined (subordinates, peers, and superiors of a focal person); for subordinates only; and for focal persons. In some cases, the sample sizes reported here may vary somewhat from those cited earlier because of differences in types of analyses and the treatment of missing values.

---

[1]Scale scores were derived by combining responses to all questionnaire items that formed a particular scale. (Responses to negatively worded items were transformed to enable addition to the positively worded items on a scale.) The number of items that made up each scale varied, thus yielding different ranges for scale scores. To simplify interpretation, the scores for each scale were therefore transformed to range from 1 to 9.

	Navy civilian personnel						High-technology firm (Avtech)						Traditional	
	Colleagues ($N = 484$)		Subordinates ($N = 179$)		Focal persons ($N = 75$)		Colleagues ($N = 386$)		Subordinates ($N = 158$)		Focal persons ($N = 60$)		Colleagues ($N = 405$)	
	Mean	SD	Mean	SD	Mean	SD	Mean	SD	Mean	SD	Mean	SD	Mean	SD
Communication style														
Careful transmitter	6.2	1.4	6.5	1.6	5.5	1.2	5.9	1.4	6.0	1.5	5.6	1.0	6.4	1.3
Open and two-way	6.1	1.4	6.0	1.7	6.4	1.1	6.0	1.4	6.1	1.5	6.4	1.0	6.6	1.3
Frank	6.4	1.4	6.4	1.5	6.0	1.2	6.4	1.3	6.6	1.3	6.3	1.2	6.6	1.3
Careful listener	7.3	1.3	7.3	1.5	6.6	1.0	7.3	1.2	7.3	1.1	6.9	.8	7.4	1.1
Informal	6.7	1.7	6.8	1.9	6.2	1.5	6.5	1.7	6.7	1.7	6.2	1.4	6.5	1.6
Credibility														
Trustworthy	7.5	1.4	7.5	1.6	7.1	1.2	7.2	1.4	7.2	1.4	6.6	1.0	7.3	1.3
Informative	7.5	1.5	7.6	1.8	7.6	1.1	7.4	1.3	7.3	1.5	7.6	.9	7.5	1.2
Dynamic	7.0	1.3	7.1	1.4	5.8	.7	7.1	1.1	7.2	1.2	5.8	.7	7.1	1.3
Outcomes														
Role clarity	7.2	1.3	7.4	1.4	6.4	1.2	7.0	1.3	7.0	1.5	6.8	1.2	7.3	1.3
Satisfaction with focal person	6.7	1.4	6.7	1.6	6.5	1.0	6.4	1.3	6.4	1.4	6.4	1.1	6.7	1.3
Job satisfaction	6.2	1.8	6.3	1.8	5.8	1.7	6.3	1.7	6.4	1.8	6.5	1.6	6.6	1.7

As noted in Chapter 2, since the number of items forming each scale varied, all the scale scores were transformed for ease of interpretation to range from 1 to 9. See Chapters 2 and 9 for further discussion concerning transformation procedures.

| production firm (Oldline) | | | | Military base | | | | | | Social service agency | | | | | |
| Subordinates (N = 198) | | Focal persons (N = 57) | | Colleagues (N = 198) | | Subordinates (N = 162) | | Focal persons (N = 38) | | Colleagues (N = 164) | | Subordinates (N = 102) | | Focal person (N = 30) | |
Mean	SD	Mean	SD	Mean	SD	Mean	SD	Mean	SD	Mean	SD	Mean	SD	Mean	SD
6.6	1.4	6.2	1.0	6.6	1.3	6.9	1.2	6.1	1.0	6.5	1.5	6.6	1.5	5.6	1.0
6.9	1.3	6.5	1.2	6.5	1.4	6.2	1.2	6.9	1.3	6.6	1.5	6.5	1.5	6.5	1.1
6.9	1.3	6.5	1.2	6.9	1.3	6.5	.9	6.4	1.2	6.4	1.4	6.5	1.4	5.9	1.2
7.4	1.2	7.5	.8	3.0	.9	2.7	.4	3.4	.8	7.7	1.2	7.6	1.3	6.7	.7
6.8	1.6	6.6	1.1	7.0	1.7	8.2	1.0	7.1	1.1	6.8	1.6	6.8	1.6	6.2	1.2
7.4	1.3	6.8	1.3	7.7	1.3	8.1	.6	7.4	1.1	7.6	1.4	7.5	1.4	6.7	.9
7.6	1.5	7.6	1.0	8.0	1.2	8.0	.7	7.8	1.3	7.6	1.5	7.5	1.8	7.1	1.1
7.3	1.3	5.8	.6	5.8	.7	5.5	.6	7.0	1.2	7.0	1.0	7.1	1.1	5.5	.7
7.3	1.4	7.0	1.1	7.6	1.0	6.8	1.5	7.2	1.0	7.3	1.3	7.3	1.5	6.8	.9
6.7	1.4	6.6	1.0	7.1	1.3	7.1	.8	7.1	1.0	6.8	1.4	6.8	1.5	6.6	.8
6.4	1.7	6.6	1.8	6.0	2.0	4.8	2.4	6.3	1.8	6.1	1.7	5.8	1.8	6.4	1.6

References

Albaum, G. Horizontal information flow: An explanatory study. *Academy of Management Journal*, 1964, *7*, 21–33.

Aldrich, H. Technology and organization structure: A reexamination of the findings of the Aston Group. *Administrative Science Quarterly*, 1972, *17*, 26–43.

Allen, T. J. Studies of the problem-solving process in engineering design. *IEEE Transactions on Engineering Management*, 1966, *EM–13* (2), 72–83.

Allen, T. J. Communications in the research and development laboratory. *Technology Review*, 1967, *70*(1), 31–37.

Allen, T. J., & Cohen, S. I. Information flow in research and development laboratories. *Administrative Science Quarterly*, 1969, *14*, 12–19.

Allen, T. J., & Gerstberger, P. G. A field experiment to improve communications in a product engineering department: The non-territorial office. *Human Factors*, 1973, *15*(5), 487–498.

Alpert, M. I., & Anderson, W. T. Optimal heterophily and communication effectiveness: Some empirical findings. *Journal of Communication*, 1973, *23*(3), 328–343.

Anderson, K. E., & Clevenger, T. A summary of experimental research in ethos, *Speech Monographs* 1963, *30*, 59–78.

Argyris, C. *Personality and organization*. New York: Harper, 1957.

Argyris, C. *Understanding organizational behavior*. Homewood, Ill.: Dorsey, 1960.

Argyris, C. *Interpersonal competence and organizational effectiveness*. Homewood, Ill.: Irwin, 1962.

Ashby, W. R. Analysis of the system to be modeled. In R. Stodgill (Ed.), *The process of model-building in the behavioral sciences*. New York: Norton and Co., 1970.

Athanassiades, J. C. The distortion of upward communication in hierarchical organizations. *Academy of Management Journal*, 1973, *16*(2), 207.

Athanassiades, J. C. An investigation of some communication patterns of female subordinates in hierarchical organizations. *Human Relations*, 1974, *27*(3), 195–209.

Bacharach, S. B., & Aiken, M. Communication in administrative bureaucracies. *Academy of Management Journal*, 1977, *20*(3), 365–377.

Baird, J. E., & Diebolt, J. C. Role congruence, communication, superior–subordinate relations, and employee satisfaction in organization hierarchies. *Western Speech Communication*, 1976, *40*(4), 260–269.

Barnard, C. I. *The functions of the executive*. Cambridge, Mass.: Harvard Univ. Press, 1938.

Barnlund, D. C. *Interpersonal communication: survey and studies*. Boston: Houghton, 1968.

Barnlund, D. C. A transactional model of communication. In J. Akin, A. Goldberg, G. Myers, & J. Stewart (Eds.), *Language behavior: A book of readings*. The Hague: Mouton and Co., 1970.

Barnlund, D. C., & Harland, C. Propinquity and prestige as determinants of communication networks. *Sociometry*, 1963, *26*, 467–479.

Bass, B. M. *Leadership, psychology and organizational behavior*. New York: Harper, 1960.

Bass, B. M. The substance and the shadow. *American Psychologist*, 1974, *29*, 870–886.

Bass, B. M. A systems survey research feedback for management and organizational development. *Journal of Applied Behavioral Science*, 1976, *12*(2), 215–229.

Bass, B. M., Burger, P., Doktor, R., & Barrett, G. *Assessment of managers: An international comparison*. New York: Free Press, 1979.

Bass, B. M., Cascio, W. R., & O'Connor, E. Magnitude estimations of expressions of frequency and amount. *Journal of Applied Psychology*, 1974, *59*(3), 313–320.

Bass, B. M., & Eldridge, L. D. Accelerated managers' objectives in twelve countries. *Industrial Relations*, 1973, *12*, 158–171.

Bass, B. M., Farrow, D. L., Valenzi, E. R., & Solomon, R. J. Management styles associated with organizational, task, personal, and interpersonal contingencies. *Journal of Applied Psychology*, 1975, *60*(6), 720–729.

Bass, B. M., & Valenzi, E. R. *Contingent aspects of effective management styles* (Tech. Rep. 67). New York: University of Rochester, Management Research Center, 1974.

Baumgartel, H. Using employee questionnaire results for improving organizations. *Kansas Business Review*, 1959, *12*, 2–7.

Bavelas, A. Communication patterns in task-oriented groups. *Journal of the Accoustical Society of America*, 1950, *22*, 725–730.

Bavelas, A., & Barrett, D. An experimental approach to organizational communication. *Personnel*, 1951, *27*, 366–371.

Berlo, D. K. *The process of communication*. New York: Holt, 1960.

Berlo, D. K., Lemert, J. B., & Mertz, R. J. Dimensions for evaluating the acceptability of message sources. *Public Opinion Quarterly*, 1969–1970, *33*(4), 563–576.

Blalock, H. M. *Causal inference in non-experimental research*. Chapel Hill, N.C.: Univ. of North Carolina Press, 1964.

Blau, P. M. Patterns of interaction among a group of officials in a government agency. *Human Relations*, 1954, *7*, 337–348.

Blau, P. M. The hierarchy of authority in organizations. *American Journal of Sociology*, 1968, *73*(4), 453–457.

Blau, P. M., & Schoenherr, R. A. *The structure of organizations.* New York: Basic Books, 1971.

Bowers, D. G. OD techniques and their results in 23 organizations: The Michigan ICL study. *Journal of Applied Behavioral Science* 1973, *9*, 21–43.

Bowers, J. W., & Phillips, W. A. A note on the generality of source-credibility scales. *Speech Monographs*, 1967, *34*(2), 185–186.

Boyle, R. P. Path analysis and ordinal data. *American Journal of Sociology*, 1970, *75*, 461–480.

Bray, D. W., Campbell, R. J., & Grant, D. L. *Formative years in business: A long-term AT&T study of managerial lives.* New York: Wiley, 1974.

Bray, D. W. & Grant, D. L. The assessment center in the measurement of potential for business management. *Psychological Monographs: General and Applied*, 1966, *80*(17), 27.

Brenner, M. H. & Sigband, N. B. Organizational communication—An analysis based on empirical data. *Academy of Management Journal*, 1973, *16*(2), 323–325.

Bricker, W. H. The Manager of today looks at those of tommorrow. Paper presented at the Conference of the Academy of Management, Seattle, 1974. (Cited in J. L. Owen, P. A. Page, & C. I. Zimmerman, *Communication in organizations.* St. Paul: West Publishing, 1976.)

Bruner, J. S., Goodnow, J. J., & Austin, G. A. *A study of thinking.* New York: Wiley, 1956.

Buening, C. R. II *Communicating on the job. A practical guide for supervisors.* Reading, Mass.: Addison-Wesley, 1974.

Burgess, R. Communication networks and behavioral consequences. *Human Relations*, 1969, *22*(2), 137–159.

Burke, R. Methods of resolving interpersonal conflict. *Personnel Administration*, 1969, (July–August), 48–55.

Burke, R., & Wilcox, D. Effects of different patterns and degrees of openness in superior–subordinate communication on subordinate job satisfaction. *Academy of Management Journal*, 1969, *12*, 319–326.

Burns, T. The directions of activity and communication in a departmental excecutive group. *Human Relations*, 1954, *7*, 73–97.

Burns, T. & Stalker, G. *The management of innovation.* Chicago: Quadrangle Books, 1961.

Carbone, T. Stylistic variables as related to source credibility: A content analysis approach. *Speech Monographs*, 1975, *42*(2), 99–106.

Carlson, S. *Executive behavior.* Stockholm: Stromborgs, 1951.

Chapanis, A. Prelude to 2001: Exploration in human communication. *American Psychologist*, 1971, *26*(11), 949–961.

Cherry, C. *On human communication: A review, a survey, and a criticism* (2nd ed.). Cambridge, Mass.: MIT Press, 1966.

Cohen, A. R. Situational structure, self-esteem, and threat-oriented reactions to power. In D. Cartwright (Ed.), *Studies in social power.* Ann Arbor: University of Michigan, Institute for Social Research, 1959.

Comstock, D. E., & Scott, W. R. Technology and the structure of subunits: Distinguishing individual and workgroup effects. *Administrative Science Quarterly*, 1977, *22*(2), 177–202.

Conrath, D. W. Communications environment and its relationship to organizational structure. *Management Science*, 1973, *20*(4), 586–603. (a)

Conrath, D. W. Communication patterns, organizational structure, and man: Some relationships. *Human Factors*, 1973, *15*(5), 459–470. (b)

Cook, J., Hepworth, S.,. Well, T., & Warr, P. *The experience of work: A compendium and review of 249 measures and their use.* New York: Academic Press, 1981.

Cyert, R. M., & March, J. G. *A behavioral theory of the firm.* Englewood Cliffs, N.J.: Prentice-Hall, 1963.

Dance, F. E. X. Toward a theory of human communication. In F. E. X. Dance (Ed.), *Human communication theory.* New York: Holt 1967.

Dance, F. E. X. The "concept" of communication. *The Journal of Communication*, 1970, *20*, 201–210.

Davis, K. Management communication and the grapevine. *Harvard Business Review*, 1953, *31*(5), 43–49.

Davis, K. Success of chain of command oral communications in a manufacturing management group. *Academy of Management Journal*, 1968, *11*(4), 379–387.

Dearborn, D., & Simon, H. Selective perception: A note on the departmental identifications of executives. *Sociometry*, 1958, *21*, 140–144.

Deutsch, M. Trust and suspicion. *Journal of Conflict Resolution* 1958, *2*, 265–279.

Dewhirst, H. D. Influence of perceived information-sharing norms on communication channel utilization. *Academy of Management Journal*, 1971, *14*(3), 305–315.

Donald, M. N. Some concomitants of varying patterns of communication in a large organization. Unpublished doctoral dissertation, University of Michigan, 1959.

Downs, C. W. The relationship between communication and job satisfaction. In R. C. Huseman, C. M. Logue, & D. L. Freshley (eds.), *Readings in interpersonal communication* (3rd ed.). Boston: Holbrook Press, Inc. 1977.

Downs, C. W. & Hazen, M. D. A factor analytic study of communication satisfaction. *Journal of Business Communication*, 1977, *14*(3), 63–73.

Duker, S. Teaching listening: Recently developed programs and materials. *Training and Development Journal*, 1970, *24*(5), 11–15.

England, G. W. *The manager and his values: An international perspective.* Cambridge, Mass.: Ballinger, 1976.

England, G. W. & Weber, M. L. Managerial success: A study of value and demographic correlates (ONR Tech. Rep.) Minneapolis: University of Minnesota, Center for the Study of Organizational Performance and Human Effectiveness, 1972.

Falcione, R. L. Credibility: Qualifier of subordinate participation. *Journal of Business Communication*, 1974, *11*(3), 43–54. (a)

Falcione, R. L. The factor structure of source credibility scales for immediate superiors in the organizational context. *Central States Speech Journal*, 1974, *25*, 63–66. (b)

Farrow, D. L., Valenzi, E. R., & Bass, B. Managerial political behavior, executive success, and effectiveness. *Proceedings of the Academy of Management*, 1981.

Fayol, H. *General and industrial management*, London: Pitman, 1949.

Festinger, L. *A theory of cognitive dissonance.* New York: Harper, 1957.

Form, W. H. Technology and social behavior of workers in four countries: A sociotechnical perspective. *American Sociological Review*, 1972, *37*, 727–738.

Friedlander, F. The primacy of trust as a facilitator of further group accomplishment. *Journal of Applied Behavioral Science*, 1970, *6*, 387–400.

Friedlander, F., & Brown, L. D. Organizational development. *Annual Review of Psychology*, 1974, *25*, 319.

Fulton, R. B. The measurement of speaker credibility. *The Journal of Communication*, 1970, *20*, 270–279.

Gerstberger, P. G., & Allen, T. J. Criteria used by research and development engineers in the selection of an information source. *Journal of Applied Psychology*, 1968, *52*(4), 272–279.

Gerwin, D. The comparative analysis of structure and technology: A critical appraisal. *Academy of Management Review*, 1979, *4*(1), 41–51.

Gibb, J. R. Climate for trust formation. In L. P. Bradford, J. R. Gibb, & K. D. Benne (Eds.), *T-group theory and laboratory method*. New York: Wiley, 1964.

Giffin, K. The contribution of studies of source credibility to a theory of interpersonal trust in the communication process. *Psychological Bulletin*, 1967, *68*(2), 104–120.

Goetzinger, C., & Valentine, M. Communication channels, media, directional flow and attitudes in an academic community. *Journal of Communication*, 1962, *12*(1), 23–26.

Goldhaber, G. M., Porter, D. J., Yates, M. P., & Lesniak, R. Organizational communication: 1978. *Human Communication Research*, 1978, *5*(1), 76–96.

Greiner, L. E. Red flags in organization development. *Business Horizons*, 1972, *15*, 17–24.

Greller, M. M., & Herold, D. M. Sources of feedback: A preliminary investigation. *Organizational Behavior and Human Performance*, 1975, *13*, 244–256.

Guetzkow, H. Communications in organizations. In J. C. March (Ed.), *Handbook of organizations*. Chicago: Rand McNally, 1965.

Guilford, J. P. *Fundamental statistics in psychology and education*. New York: McGraw-Hill, 1965.

Gulick. L., & Urwick, L. (Eds.). *Papers on scientific administration*. New York: Columbia University, Institute of Public Administration, 1937.

Gullahorn, J. T. Distance and friendship as factors in the gross interaction matrix. *Sociometry*, 1952, *15*, 123–134.

Hage, J. *Communication and organizational control: Cybernetics in health and welfare settings*. New York: Wiley, 1974.

Hage, J., Aiken, M., & Marrett, C. Organizational structure and communications. *American Sociological Review*, 1971, *36*(5), 860–871.

Hall, R., Haas, J. E., & Johnson, N. J. Organizational size, complexity, and formalization. *American Sociological Review*, 1967, *32*(6), 903–912.

Haney, W. V. *Communication and organizational behavior: Text and cases* (3rd ed.). Homewood, Ill.: Irwin, 1973.

Hanser, L. M., & Muchinsky, P. M. Work as an information environment. *Organizational Behavior and Human Performance*, 1978, *21*, 47–60.

Harman, H. H. *Modern factor analysis*. Chicago: Univ. of Chicago Press, 1967.

Hawkins, B. L., & Penley, L. The relationship of communication to performance and satisfaction. Paper presented at the meetings of the Academy of Management, San Francisco, 1978.

Hays, W. *Statistics*, New York: Holt, 1963.

Hegarty, W. H. Supervisor's reactions to subordinates' appraisals. *Personnel*, 1973, *50*, 30–35.

Hegarty, W. H. Using subordinate ratings to elicit behavioral changes in supervisors. *Journal of Applied Psychology*, 1974, *59*, 764–766.

Hickson, D. J., Pugh, D. S., & Pheysey, D. C. Operations technology and organization structure: An empirical reappraisal. *Administrative Science Quarterly*, 1969, *14*(3), 378–397.

Holland, W. E. Information potential: A concept of the importance of information sources in a research development environment. *The Journal of Communication*, 1972, *22*, 150–173.

House, R. J., & Rizzo, J. R. Role conflict and ambiguity as critical variables in a model of organization behavior. *Organizational Behavior and Human Performance*, 1972, *7*, 467–505.

Housel, T. J., & Davis, W. E., The reduction of upward communication distortion. *Journal of Business Communication*, 1977, *14*(4), 49–65.

Hovland, C. I., Janis, I. L. & Kelley, H. H. *Communication and persuasion*. New Haven: Yale Univ. Press, 1953.

Huseman, R. C., Lahiff, J. M., & Hatfield, J. D. *Interpersonal communication in organizations: A perceptual approach*. Boston: Holbrook Press, Inc., 1976.

Huysmans, J. *The implementation of operations research*. New York: Wiley, 1970.

Indik, B. P., Georgopoulos, B. S., & Seashore, S. E. Superior–subordinate relationships and performance. *Personnel Psychology*, 1961, *14*, 357–374.

Jain, H. C. Supervisory communication and performance in urban hospitals. *Journal of Communication*, 1973, *23*(1), 103–117.

Johnson, F. C., & Klare, G. R. General models of communication research: A survey of the developments of a decade. *Journal of Communication*, 1961, *11*, 13–26.

Johnston, J. *Econometric methods* New York: McGraw-Hill, 1963.

Julian, J. Compliance patterns and communication blocks in complex organizations. *American Sociological Review*, 1966, *31*(3), 382–389.

Kahn, R. L., Wolfe, D. M., Quinn, R. P., Snock, J. D., & Rosenthanl, R. A. *Organizational stress*. New York: Wiley, 1964.

Katz, D. & Kahn, R. *The social psychology of organizations*. New York: Wiley, 1966.

Katz, D., & Kahn, R. *The social psychology of organizations* (2nd ed.). New York: Wiley, 1978.

Katz, R., & Tushman, M. Communication patterns, project performance and task characteristics: An empirical evaluation and integration in an R&D setting. *Organizational Behavior and Human Performance*, 1979, *23*, 139–162.

Keefe, W. F. *Listen management*. New York: McGraw-Hill, 1971.

Keller, R., & Holland, W. E. Individual characteristics of innovativeness and communication in research and development organizations. *Journal of Applied Psychology*, 1978, *63*(6), 759–762.

Kerlinger, F. N., & Pedhauzer, E. L. *Multiple regression in behavioral research*. New York: Holt, 1973.

Kimberly, J. R. Organizational size and the structuralist perspective: A review, critique, and proposal. *Administrative Science Quarterly*, 1976, *21*(4), 571–597.

Labovitz, S. Some observations on measurement and statistics. *Social Forces*, 1967, *46*, 151–160.

Labovitz, S. In defense of assigning numbers to ranks. *American Sociological Review*, 1970, *35*, 515–524.

Lasswell, H. D. The structure and function of communication in society. In L. Bryson (Ed.), *The Communication of ideas*. New York: Harper, 1948.

Laurent, H. *Predicting managerial success.* Ann Arbor: Foundation for Research and Human Behavior, 1968.

Lawler, E. E., III, Porter, L. W., & Tennenbaum, A. Managers' attitudes toward interaction episodes. *Journal of Applied Psychology*, 1968, *52*, 423–439.

Lawrence, A. C. Individual differences in work motivation. *Human Relations*, 1972, *25*(4), 327–335.

Lawrence, P., & Lorsch, J. *Organization and environment*. Cambridge, Mass.: Harvard University Press, 1967.

Lawson, E. Change in communication nets, performance, and morale. *Human Relations*, 1965, *18*, 139–147.

Leavitt, H. J. Some effects of certain communication patterns on group performance. *Journal of Abnormal and Social Psychology*, 1951, *46*, 38–50.

Lee, I. J., & Lee, L. L. *Handling barriers in communication*. New York: Harper, 1956.

Level, D. A. Communication effectiveness: Method and situation. *Journal of Business Communication*, 1972, *10*, 19–25.

Level, D. A. & Johnson, L. Accuracy of information flows within the superior/ subordinate relationship. *Journal of Business Communication*, 1978, *15*(2), 12–22.

Likert, R. *New patterns of management*. New York: McGraw-Hill, 1961.

Likert, R. *The human organization*. New York: McGraw-Hill, 1967.

Luthans, F. *Organizational behavior*. New York: McGraw-Hill, 1973.

Lyons, M. Techniques for using ordinal measures in regression and path analysis. In H. L. Costner (Ed.), *Sociological methodology*. San Franciso: Jossey-Bass, 1971.

Maloney. P. W., & Hinrichs, J. R. A new tool for supervisory self-development. *Personnel*, 1959, *36*, 46–53.

Mandell, M. Supervisory characteristics and ratings: A summary of recent research. *Personnel*, 1956, *32*, 435–440.

March, J. G., & Simon, H. A. *Organizations*. New York: Wiley, 1958.

Mason, R. O. & Mitroff, I. I. A program for research on management information systems. *Management Science*, 1973, *19*(5), 475–487.

McCroskey, J. C. Scales for the measurement of ethos. *Speech Monographs* 1966, *33*(1), 65–72.

McGregor, D. *The human side of enterprise*. New York: McGraw-Hill, 1960.

McKenney, J. L. Computer based models as adaptive communications between different cognitive styles, In C. H. Kriebel, R. L. VanHorn, & J. T. Heames (Ed.), *Management information systems: progress and perspective*. Pittsburgh, Pa.: Carnegie Press, 1971.

Meehl, P. Theory testing in psychology and physics. *Philosophy of Science* 1967, *34*, 103–115.

Mellinger, G. D. Interpersonal trust as a factor in communication. *Journal of Abnormal and Social Psychology, 1956, 52*, 304–309.

Merton, R. K. *Social theory and social structure*. New York: Free Press, 1957.

Mintzberg, H. *The nature of managerial work*. New York: Harper, 1973.

Mock, T. J. A longitudinal study of some information structure alternatives. In *Proceedings of the Wharton Conference on Research on Computers in Organizations*, October 24–25, 1973.

Mohr, L. B. Organizational technology and organization structure. *Administrative Science Quarterly*, 1971, *16*(4), 444–459.

Monge, P. R., Edwards, J. A., & Kirste, K. K. The determinants of communication and communication structure in large organizations: A review of research. In B. Ruben (Ed.), *Communication yearbook 2*. New Brunswick, N.J.: Transaction Books, 1978.

Monge, P. R., & Kirste, K. K. Proximity, location, time and opportunity to communicate (ONR tech. Rep. 3, Contract No. N00014–73–A–0476–0001). San Jose: California State University, 1975.

Mooney, J. D., & Reiley, A. C. *The principles of organization*. New York: Harper, 1939.

Morris, C. W. *Signs, language and behavior*. Englewood Cliffs, N.J.: Prentice-Hall, 1946.

Murray, M. A. Education for public administration *Public Personnel Management*. 1976 *5*(4), 239–249.

Nadler, D. A. *Feedback and organization development: Using data-based methods*. Reading, Mass.: Addison-Wesley, 1977.

Newcomb, T. M. An approach to the study of communicative acts. *Psychological Review*, 1953, *60*, 393–404.

Newell, A., Shaw, J. C., & Simon, H. A. Elements of theory of human program solving. *Psychological Review*, 1958, *65*, 151–166.

Nichols, R. G. ,& Stevens, L. A. Listening to people. *Harvard Business Review*, 1957, *35*(5), 85–92.

Nie, N., Hull, C., Jenkins, J., Steinbrenner, K., & Bent, D. *Statistical package for the social sciences* (2nd ed.). New York: McGraw-Hill, 1975.

Nunnally, J. C. *Psychometric theory*. New York: McGraw-Hill, 1967.

O'Reilly, C. A. Supervisors and peers as information sources, group supportiveness, and individual decision-making performance. *Journal of Applied Psychology*, 1977, *62*(5), 632–635.

O'Reilly, C. A. The intentional distortion of information in organizational communication: A laboratory and field investigation. *Human Relations*, 1978, *31*(2), 173–193.

O'Reilly, C. A., & Roberts, K. H. Information filtration in organizations: Three experiments. *Organizational Behavior and Human Performance*, 1974, *11*, 253–265.

O'Reilly, C. A., & Roberts, K. Relationships among components of credibility and communication behaviors in work units. *Journal of Applied Psychology*, 1976, *61*(1), 99–102.

O'Reilly, C. A., & Roberts, K. Task group structure, communication, and effectiveness in three organizations. *Journal of Applied Psychology*, 1977, *62*(6), 674–681.

Pascale, R. T. Communication and decision-making across cultures: Japanese and American companies. *Administrative Science Quarterly*, 1978, *23*, 91–110.

Pelz, D. C., & Andrews, F. M. *Scientists in organizations* (rev. ed.). Ann Arbor: Institute for Social Research, University of Michigan, 1976.

Penley, L. E. Organizational communication: Its relationship to the structure of work groups. In R. C. Huseman, C. M. Logue, & D. L. Freshley, *Readings in interpersonal and organizational communication*. Boston: Holbrook Press, Inc., 1977.

Petrie, C. R. Informative speaking: A summary and bibliography of related research. *Speech Monographs*, 1963, *30*(2) 79–98.

Pfeffer, J., & Salancik, G. R. *The external control of organizations*. New York: Harper, 1978.

Popper, K. R. *The logic of scientific discovery*. London: Hutchinson and Co., Ltd., 1959.

Porter, L. W., & Lawler, E. E. Properties of organization structure in relation to job attitudes and job behavior. *Psychological Bulletin*, 1965, *64*, 23–51.

Porter, L. W. & Roberts, K. H. Communication in organizations. In M. Dunnette (Ed.), *Handbook of industrial and organizational psychology*. Chicago: Rand McNally, 1976.

Price, J. L. *Organizational effectiveness, an inventory of propositions*. Homewood, Ill.: Irwin, 1968,

Price, J. L. *The study of turnover.* Ames: Iowa State Univ. Press, 1977.

Randolph, W. A., & Finch, F. E. The relationship between organization technology and the direction and frequency dimensions of task communications. *Human Relations*, 1977, *30*(12), 1131–1145.

Read, W. H. Upward communication in industrial hierarchies. *Human Relations*, 1962, *15*, 3–15.

Rizzo, J. R., House, R. J. & Lirtzman, S. I. Role conflict and ambiguity in complex organizations. *Administrative Science Quarterly*, 1970, *15*, 150–163.

Roberts, D. F. The nature of human communication effects. In W. Schramm & D. F. Roberts (Eds.), *Process and effects of mass communication* (rev. ed.). Urbana: Univ. of Illinois Press, 1971.

Roberts, K. H., & O'Reilly, C. A. Empirical findings and suggestions for future research on organizational communication (ONR Tech. Rep. (Interim) Contract No. N000314–69–A–0200–1054). Irvine, Calif.: University of California. August 1974. (a)

Roberts, K. H., & O'Reilly, C. A. Failures in upward communication in organizations. *Academy of Management Journal*, 1974, *17*, 205–215. (b)

Roberts, K. H., & O'Reilly, C. A. Measuring organizational communication. *Journal of Applied Psychology*, 1974, *39*(3), 321–326. (c)

Roberts, K. H., O'Reilly, C. A., Bretton, G. E., and Porter, L. W. Organizational theory and organizational communication: a communication failure? *Human Relations*, 27(5), 501–524.

Roethlisberger, F. J. & Dickson, W. J. *Management and the worker.* Cambridge, Mass.: Harvard Univ. Press, 1939.

Rogers, C. R. & Roethlisberger, F. J. Barriers and gateways to communication. *Harvard Business Review*, 1952, *30*(4), 46–52.

Rogers, E. M. & Agarwala-Rogers, R. *Communication in organizations.* New York: Free Press, 1976.

Rogers, E. M. & Bhowmik, D. K. Homophily–heterophily: Relational concepts for communication research. *Public Opinion Quarterly*, 1971, *34*, 523–538.

Rozeboom, W. W. *Foundations of the theory of prediction.* Homewood, Ill.: Dorsey Press, 1966.

Schein, E. H. *Process consultation: Its role in organization development.* Reading, Mass.: Addison-Wesley, 1969.

Schreisheim, C. A., Kinicki, A. J., & Schreisheim, J. F. The effect of leniency on leader behavior descriptions. *Organizational Behavior and Human Performance*, 1979, *23*, 1–29.

Schroder, H. M., Driver, M. J., & Streufert, S. *Human information processing.* New York: Holt, 1967.

Shannon, C. A mathematical theory of communication. *Bell System Technical Journal*, 1948, *27*, 379–423, 623–656.

Shannon, C., & Weaver, W. *The mathematical theory of communication.* Urbana: Univ. of Illinois Press, 1949.

Shaw, M. E. Some effects of problem complexity upon problem solution efficiency in different communication nets. *Journal of Experimental Psychology*, 1954, *48*, 211–217.

Shaw, M. Communication networks. In L. Berkowitz (Ed.), *Advances in experimental social psychology* (Vol. 1). New York: Academic Press, 1964.

Simon, H. A. *Administrative behavior.* New York: Macmillan, 1945.

Simon, H. A behavioral model of rational choice. *Quarterly Journal of Economics*, 1955, *69*, 99–118.

Simon, H. Rational choice and the structure of environment. *Psychological Review*, 1956, *63*, 129–138.

Simon, H. *Models of man.* New York: Wiley, 1957.

Simons, H. W., Berkowitz, N. N. & Moyer, R. J. Similarity, credibility, and attitude change: A review and a theory. *Psychological Bulletin*, 1970, *73*(1), 1–16.

Smith, E. E. The effect of clear and unclear role expectations on group productivity and defensiveness. *Journal of Abnormal and Social Psychology*, 1957, *55*, 213–217.

Smith, P. C., Kendall, L. M., & Hulin, C. L., *The measurement of satisfaction in work and retirement.* Chicago: Rand NcNally, 1969.

Snadowsky, A. M. Communication network research: An examination of controversies. *Human Relations*, 1972, *25*(4), 283–306.

Solomon, R. *The importance of manager–subordinate perceptual differences to the study of leadership.* Unpublished doctoral dissertation, University of Rochester, 1975.

Solomon, R. J. An examination of the relationship between a survey feedback O.D. technique and the work environment. *Personnel Psychology*, 1976, *29*, 583–594.

Stogdill, R. S. *Handbook of leadership.* New York: Free Press, 1974.

Sutton, H., & Porter, L. W. A study of the grapevine in a governmental organization. *Personnel Psychology*, 1968, *21*, 223–230.

Taylor, F. *Scientific management.* New York: Harper, 1911.

Thayer, L. Communication and organization theory. In F. E. X. Dance (Ed.), *Human communication theory.* New York: Holt, 1967.

Thayer, L. *Communication and communication systems.* Homewood: Irwin, 1968.

Thomas, E. J., & Fink, C. F. Effects of group size. *Psychological Bulletin*, 1963, *60*(4), 371–384.

Thompson, J. D. *Organizations in action.* New York: McGraw-Hill, 1967.

Tolman, E. *Purposive behavior in animals and men.* New York: Appleton, 1932.

Tolman, E. & Brunswik, E. The organism and the causal texture of the environment. *Psychological Review*, 1935, *42*, 43–77.

Triandis, H. C. Cognitive similarity and interpersonal communication in industry. *Journal of Applied Psychology*, 1959, *43*(5), 321–326.

Tushman, M. L. Special boundary roles in the innovation process. *Administrative Science Quarterly*, 1977, *22*, 587–605.

Tushman, M. Technical communication in R & D laboratories: The impact of project work characteristics. *Academy of Management Journal*, 1978, *21*(4), 624–645.

Underwood, W. O. A hospital director's administrative profile. *Hospital Administration*, 1963, 37–39.

Van de Ven, A., Delbecq, A., & Koenig, R. Determinants of coordination modes within organizations. *American Sociological Review*, 1976, *41*, 322–338.

Walton, E. Motivation to communicate. *Personnel Administration*, 1962, *25*(2), 17–19.

Walton, E. A study of organizational communication systems. *Personnel Administration*, 1963, *26*(3), 46–49.

Weber, M. *The theory of social and economic organization* (Henderson and Parsons Translation). Oxford: Oxford Univ. Press, 1947.

Weick, K. *The social psychology of organizing.* Reading, Mass.: Addison-Wesley, 1969.

Weinshall, T. D. (Ed.). *Managerial communication: Concepts, approaches and techniques.* New York: Academic Press, 1979.

Weinshall, T. D. & Shalev, M. A dynamic approach to the study of managerial structure and interpersonal interaction. In T. D. Weinshall (Ed.), *Managerial communication: Concepts, approaches and techniques.* New York: Academic Press, 1979.

Weisbord, M. R. Organizational diagnosis: Six places to look for trouble with or without a theory. *Group and Organizational Studies*, 1976, *1*(4), 430–447.

Westley, B. H. & Maclean, M. S. A conceptual model for communications research. *Journalism Quarterly*, 1957, *34*, 31–38.

Whitley, R., & Frost, P. Task type and information transfer in a government research laboratory. *Human Relations*, 1973, *25*(4), 537–550.

Wickesberg, A. K. Communication networks in the business organization structure. *Academy of Management Journal*, 1968, *11*, 256–268.

Wilensky, H. L. *Organizational intelligence: Knowledge and policy in government and industry.* New York: Basic Books, 1967.

Wofford, J. C., Gerloff, E. A., & Cummins, R. C. *Organizational communication.* New York: McGraw-Hill, 1977.

Woodward, J. *Industrial organization: Theory and practice.* New York: Oxford Univ. Press, 1965.

Zand, D. E. Trust and managerial problem solving. *Administrative Science Quarterly*, 1972, *17*(2), 229–239.

Index